PRAISE FOR
EMOTIONALLY INVESTED

"Financial happiness stems less from numbers and investing jargon and more from understanding fears of missing out or running out. In *Emotionally Invested,* Mary Evans offers entertaining and insightful financial therapy to convert your 'Money Whys' into becoming money wise."

—Gregory Karp, veteran business journalist and author of *Living Rich by Spending Smart* **and** *The 1-2-3 Money Plan*

"*Emotionally Invested* dives into the emotions behind financial decisions, revealing how emotions shape our relationship with money in ways we often overlook. Through relatable stories and practical insights, it highlights the importance of understanding emotional triggers to make sound financial choices. It is a must read for anyone looking to gain control over their finances and financial happiness by first understanding themselves."

—Marilyn Bauer, retired IBM manager

"*Emotionally Invested* is a creative and easy read. Entertaining, informative, and thought-provoking. A subject most of us try to avoid … but know we can't."

—Jack Peters, CEO, JR Peters Inc.

EMOTIONALLY INVESTED

MARY CLEMENTS EVANS

CFP®, CDFA®, ABFP®

EMOTIONALLY INVESTED

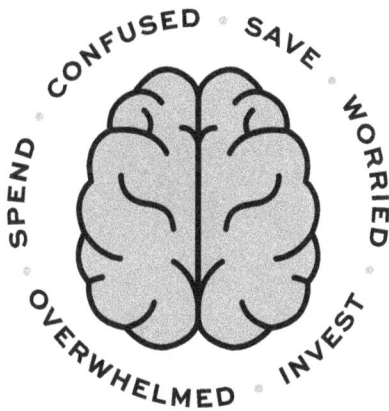

SPEND · CONFUSED · SAVE · WORRIED · INVEST · OVERWHELMED

OUTSMART YOUR ANXIETY FOR
FEARLESS RETIREMENT PLANNING

Forbes | Books

Published by Forbes Books, Charleston, South Carolina.
An imprint of Advantage Media Group.

Forbes Books is a registered trademark, and the Forbes Books colophon is a trademark of Forbes Media, LLC.

Printed in the United States of America.

10 9 8 7 6 5 4 3 2 1

ISBN: 979-8-88750-683-8 (Hardcover)
ISBN: 979-8-88750-684-5 (eBook)

Library of Congress Control Number: 2025900565

Book design by Megan Elger.

This custom publication is intended to provide accurate information and the opinions of the author in regard to the subject matter covered. It is sold with the understanding that the publisher, Forbes Books, is not engaged in rendering legal, financial, or professional services of any kind. If legal advice or other expert assistance is required, the reader is advised to seek the services of a competent professional.

Since 1917, Forbes has remained steadfast in its mission to serve as the defining voice of entrepreneurial capitalism. Forbes Books, launched in 2016 through a partnership with Advantage Media, furthers that aim by helping business and thought leaders bring their stories, passion, and knowledge to the forefront in custom books. Opinions expressed by Forbes Books authors are their own. To be considered for publication, please visit **books.Forbes.com**.

01-29-2025 10:21

To my beloved lost son, Dan,
whose brilliance and humor I miss every day.

CONTENTS

PART I: THE DECEPTIONS

PART II: THE EMOTIONS

DISCLAIMER

The information contained in this book does not purport to be a complete description of the securities, markets, or developments referred to in this material. The information has been obtained from sources considered to be reliable, but we do not guarantee that the foregoing material is accurate or complete. Any information provided is not a complete summary or statement of all available data necessary for making an investment decision and does not constitute a recommendation. Any opinions are those of the author and not necessarily those of Raymond James. Expressions of opinion are as of the initial book publishing date and are subject to change without notice.

Securities offered through Raymond James Financial Services, Inc., member of FINRA/SIPC. Investment advisory services offered through Raymond James Financial Services Advisors, Inc. Evans Wealth Strategies is not a registered broker/dealer and is independent of Raymond James Financial Services.

The examples used in this book are hypothetical in nature and are meant for illustrative purposes only. Future performance cannot be guaranteed, and investment yields will fluctuate with market conditions. Actual investor results will vary. Please consult with your financial advisor if you have questions about these examples and how they relate to your own financial situation.

The Certified Financial Planner Board of Standards, Inc., owns the certification marks CFP®, CERTIFIED FINANCIAL PLANNER®, the CFP® certification mark (with plaque design) in the United States, which it authorizes for use by individuals who successfully complete the CFP Board's initial and ongoing certification requirements.

The preceding book reviews are not related to the author's role as a financial advisor, are not based on performance, are not an endorsement, and may not be representative of individual clients' experience.

PART I
THE DECEPTIONS

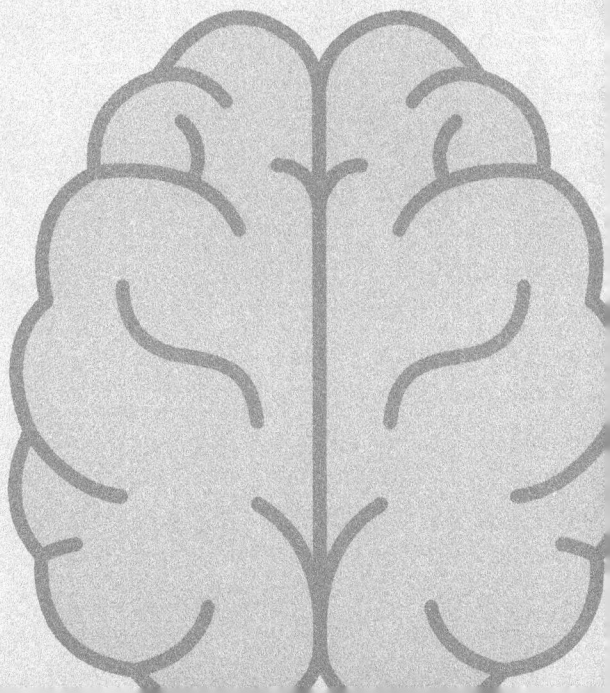

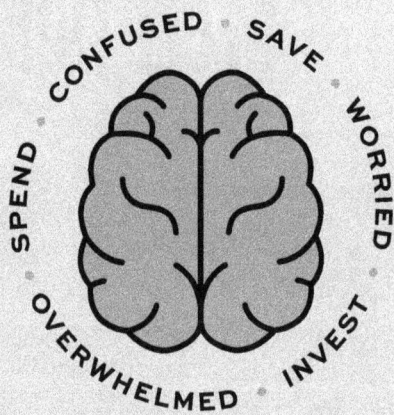

SPEND · CONFUSED · SAVE · WORRIED · INVEST · OVERWHELMED

CHAPTER 1
MY WHY

In the middle of difficulty lies opportunity.
—ALBERT EINSTEIN

What made me become a financial advisor?

I bet it's not what you think! Most folks believe that all financial advisors come from wealthy families who spend their summers yachting off the coast of Nantucket. That is *not* my story. I grew up in Hilltown, Pennsylvania, and the only boat my family had was a small red one that floated in our bathtub—the tub that, once filled, bathed all five of us kids one after the other.

Here's a photo that my dad took in front of our house on Clearview Road. It was a former chicken coop that he'd fixed up and added on to. That's me, the youngest, in front of the huge Blessed Mary statue in our front yard.

SEP 1961

Where you start is not where you finish.

My family may have been poor, but we were rich in love and laughter. My parents were the smartest, kindest, and hardest-working people I knew. But sometimes circumstances eclipse all that. My dad was a tool and die maker for the Budd Company in Philadelphia. One day, a two-ton piece of machinery fell on his leg and broke it, and things got tough. At one point we were on welfare and receiving government surplus food. (No food stamps back then.) I vividly remember my mother's tears when we had to accept these handouts. I never asked, but knowing Mom, I assumed she was crying out of sadness and shame. I knew then I didn't want that to ever be me. And through many wonderful circumstances it wasn't.

I had a terrific career in the finance departments of corporate America, working for General Battery (before it became Exide),

Kellogg's, Goodall Rubber, and, finally, Rodale Press. But after almost thirty years, at age forty-nine, I was downsized. I had seen the writing on the wall at Rodale, so I wasn't surprised, and I received a great severance package. I spent the summer floating in the pool with my girlfriends, drinking champagne.

After turning down offers to return to corporate America, a large firm offered me a job as a financial advisor. I had thought about doing that before because friends and coworkers had always asked me for financial advice, but I never thought of making it my profession or knew what it would entail. When I was offered a job doing this, I was dismayed when I quickly learned I was supposed to cold-call people and sell them a stock or a bond. I couldn't do that. In fact, I refused to do that. I had helped large companies become financially successful, and now I wanted to help families and small businesses do the same. I realized I needed to start my own company—one where I wasn't told to sell this or that, one where I could help all types of people, not just certain clients.

Thank God for Chocolate Martinis

And that's exactly what I did, founding Evans Wealth Strategies in 2008. I leased and renovated a nine-hundred-square-foot house (not unlike the one I grew up in) on the main drag of equally small Emmaus, Pennsylvania, and hung out my shingle. I had zero clients, zero assets under management, and one employee—a young woman named Crystal. Then, two weeks later, Lehman Brothers collapsed, and the Great Recession got even worse.

I can't begin to tell you how stressful this time was. It was the most volatile period in recent financial history. I was trying to ease people's fears about the markets, explaining that we were not in another depression, while working sixty to seventy hours a week without drawing a salary. After one particularly hard day, at maybe seven or eight in the evening, Crystal turned to me and asked, "Would you like me to make you a chocolate martini?"

"That sounds terrible," I said.

But Crystal insisted, and the drink was delicious! For better or worse, at the end of those tough weeks, the only items in the dishwasher were martini glasses. Crystal's chocolate martinis helped us keep our sense of humor, and during those first three months, I think I only cried once.

Slowly, the business started to grow. By the end of my first year, I had thirty clients, and despite all the hardship, I knew I'd found my purpose—or as author Simon Sinek calls it, my "why." I was helping people get the peace of mind my parents never had.

Learning to Listen Instead of Lecture

When I started as a financial advisor, I thought I would be a natural at the job. After all, I'd worked in finance at Fortune 500 companies. I'd reported to Wall Street. I understood stocks, bonds, and investments. And most importantly, I believed that everyone was just one chart, graph, or Excel spreadsheet away from achieving Financial Happiness.

But my world wasn't my clients' world. They didn't get what I was saying, and I didn't understand how they made—or responded to—financial decisions. I'd thought I would just tell them what they should do, they would do it, and they'd be happy and grateful. How arrogant and stupid of me!

I was in an industry with a long history of lecturing people. Why not, right? Doesn't everyone enjoy a good lecture, especially one full of words, acronyms, and concepts they've never heard of? Let's take a topic that makes people uncomfortable and toss in communication that makes them feel stupid and embarrassed. What could go wrong?

It's not that I didn't attract clients. I did. But I could tell they didn't understand the plan. They stayed with me because they told themselves, "Well, she seems smart." After all, I used lots of words they didn't know! But this did not put people on the path to Financial Happiness and peace of mind. It put them on the path of "At least I'm doing something."

The good news is, I'm a quick study. I threw away every book I read on how to be a financial advisor and just started talking to people. I mean *really* talking to people. And I learned to ask questions.

I quickly realized two important things:

1. Most people want to poke their eyes out when you start showing them charts, graphs, and Excel spreadsheets.

2. Most people aren't meeting their financial goals because of their relationship with money. It's not that they lack knowledge. It's that they don't grasp *why* they did or didn't make certain financial decisions.

So, I learned you can't be an effective financial advisor without delving into people's worries, fears, and relationship with money. In other words, their *Money Why*. In fact, the top reason for client satisfaction with financial advisors is not exceptional portfolio performance but rather feeling that "me and my goals" are deeply understood (see survey).

SURVEY SAYS

THE STATE OF CLIENT/ADVISOR RELATIONSHIPS*

% of clients who switched or contemplated changing advisors in 2023 = **75%**

% of clients who did so between 2020 and 2022 = **47%**

Confidence in financial plan among clients contacted frequently by advisor = **71%**

Confidence in financial plan among clients contacted infrequently or rarely = **22%**

Advisor characteristics that influence overall client satisfaction:

Deep understanding of me and my goals = **56%**

Portfolio performance = **55%**

Financial advice given = **52%**

Accessibility/availability = **48%**

Breadth of services = **45%**

Fees charged = **43%**

From a survey of 775 US respondents with professional financial advisors conducted by YCharts in 2024[1]

1   "Advisor—Client Communication Survey," YCharts, 2024, https://go.ycharts.com/hubfs/YCharts_Advisor_Client_Communication_Survey_2024.pdf.

From then on, I started experimenting with a completely different way of interacting with clients. I had no mentor or example to follow. It felt like I was creating the wheel. It wasn't easy, but it quickly became extremely rewarding—for them *and* for me. My intent was to create an environment where people would never feel shame, blame, or guilt about money. I wanted them to look forward to our meetings. I talked in analogies (so many analogies) so they could tie something they didn't understand to something they did. If my client was married, I insisted both partners be at every meeting. The result of this holistic approach was that my clients referred friends and family to me, and my business grew very quickly. But that wasn't my measure of success. It was knowing that people were meeting their goals and that they could have an open and easy conversation about money with me and with each other.

Some years later, I learned there is an official name for the approach I was taking: behavioral finance. It's based on behavioral *science*—the study of human behavior through experimentation and observation. The thing is, what we've learned about how humans actually behave is rarely applied to finance. Most money advisors (then and now) abide by the rational man theory: if you give people enough info, they'll make a highly rational decision. That's insane! We are human beings—we are never purely rational. Emotions play a huge role in everything we do. So, the field of behavioral *finance* was born. It's the reason my practice grew so fast, and my clients responded so well. I helped them identify and understand their Money Why—the underlying reasons behind their financial actions—and things finally made sense to them.

I have earned an Accredited Behavioral Finance Professional (ABFP®) certification. My goal is to deliver high-net-worth services to medium-net-worth people and, by doing so, empower them to become smarter savers and investors so they can ultimately enjoy a more secure and worry-free retirement. After more than two decades of "financial therapy," as I prefer to call it, I decided to write this book. It's intended for individuals and couples who feel frustrated and overwhelmed by money and have a hard time talking about it. And believe me, that's *a lot* of people.

Instead of telling you what stocks or mutual funds to buy, this book contains my most important observations from working with more than five hundred individuals and families for over twenty years. Chief among them is the different Money Whys people bring to the table, how these Money Whys subconsciously affect financial decisions, and, most important, how you can identify yours (and your partner's). Knowing your Money Why can change your financial world—and no, I'm not exaggerating.

There are three parts to this path (and the book):

1. *The Deceptions.* The frustration, guilt, and fear you're feeling about your financial situation are not your fault. You're not stupid. You don't deserve to be yelled at. There's no need to apologize. Government policies, economic conditions, and the rise of social media put you in this position. Realizing this will instantly ease your stress.

2. *The Emotions.* There are two primary Money Whys: FOMO (fear of missing out) and FORO (fear of running out). Once you determine yours (and your partner's), your relationship with money will become clear, talking about money will get easier, and you'll make better financial decisions.

3. *The Solutions.* I'll show you how to build a plan, based on your Money Why, that will help you achieve greater Financial Happiness.

Beware the Rug Puller

All this probably sounds terrific. Wow! Three easy steps! But it's never that simple. Life tends to pull the rug out from under us when we least expect it. This book is also about dealing with those tough times.

When my son was five, my husband was offered a great job as the chief financial officer at a company in another town. He talked me into quitting my job and staying home with our son. We moved, bought a lovely home, and joined the country club. I thought, *This is what they mean by living high off the hog.* Well, the hog died. My husband lost his job due to an unhealthy relationship with alcohol (although I didn't know that then), and it was all back on me. We had a mortgage, we hadn't been saving, and I felt like an idiot. How had I not seen this coming? After feeling poor for almost my whole life, when I finally felt rich, I'd had the rug pulled out from under me. I swore I would never rely on anyone ever again. I had to be responsible for my financial life. Me. Just me.

I was devastated, angry, and scared. I was thirty-five years old. I'd had a good career, and I knew I could do it again. But I didn't want to be far from my son. I took a job at a local company (Rodale) that was within walking distance of his school. My starting salary was about what my bonus had been at my previous job. This is where growing up poor came in handy. I had trained for the Cheapskate Olympics! So I got by. I didn't have to sell the house, and I started to save. I eventually worked my way up to vice president of finance. With a good income, I wasn't foolish enough to feel rich again. I was always frightened that the darn rug would be pulled out when I wasn't looking. And it was. The company was failing, and I was laid off.

Now what was I going to do? That's when I started my business. After ten years, *Forbes* recognized me as a Best in State and Top

Woman in State financial advisor, and I was named to the Raymond James' Chairman's Council.[2] But during those years, the rug puller showed up many times.

Five years after starting the business, my husband and I went our separate ways. It was very amicable. He even remained my client, but divorce is always painful and difficult. I recentered myself and kept moving forward. Three years later, I was diagnosed with breast cancer. It was my second cancer diagnosis. At first, I was pissed. *I've worked so hard to get here, and now the rug is pulled out again!*

I collected myself and attacked cancer like I would anything else. It was early, and I was lucky. I had surgery, and the doctors were confident they'd gotten it all. They recommended chemo and radiation. I turned down chemo but agreed to the radiation. I scheduled it for 7:30 a.m. so I wouldn't miss work. I was doing great! *I got this! What's that I see by the door? Are you kidding me? Another damn rug?* No one, and I mean no one, bothered to tell me that around week three or four, radiation knocks the stuffing out of you. I couldn't believe how tired I felt. I was so fortunate to have a fantastic staff that helped and supported me in every possible way.

Shortly after that, my son, Dan, came to work with me to train as a financial advisor. He sailed through his tests and was going to start studying to become a Certified Financial Planner® professional. I was so proud of him! He and his wife had just had their second daughter. Two of the cutest kids you ever saw. I had it all. A great company, two darling grandkids, and a new man in my life named Paul. This is why you fight and work so hard—to enjoy these rewards. Or do you?

---

2   Raymond James' Chairman's Council membership is based on prior fiscal year production. Requalification is required annually. The ranking may not be representative of any one client's experience, is not an endorsement, and is not indicative of an advisor's future performance. No fee is paid in exchange for this award/rating.

Another day, another rug. Dan and I were just finishing a meeting with a client. As we escorted her out of my office, Dan collapsed and started having a seizure. He was rushed to the hospital, where they did a brain scan. It was brain cancer. He passed away in 2022.

People often ask me how I keep going forward. I explain that having this business is one of the greatest blessings of my life. People are counting on me. I have to be there for them. But the return I get is tenfold. The love and support I receive from my clients and my team is unbelievable. It's a strange experience to feel so brokenhearted and so loved at the same time.

I know struggle, I know poverty, and I know pain. My goal in life and with this book is to help alleviate those things for you—or at least make sure you have a safety net when the rug puller comes to call.

The title of this book is *Emotionally Invested*. I picked that title because money is emotional. Understanding this is the key to finally getting to the root of your money woes and eventually achieving greater Financial Happiness in retirement. I've found that people don't want to be billionaires. (Well, most don't.) They don't care if Warren Buffett is short on corn futures. They just want to feel financially secure and stop worrying about money. Identifying *why* you handle money the way you do and *why* you're in your current financial situation can be a life-changing experience. I know. I see it every day.

Today, Evans Wealth Strategies has nine employees (including Crystal!), I manage over half a billion dollars in assets, and I'm headquartered in a spacious former gym that's nearly ten times the size of my original office. (In a sweet twist of fate, I bought the gym from the company that laid me off!) Plus, I've been nationally recognized for my work with clients. And I'm happily remarried.

I'm living proof that while the rug puller is persistent, he doesn't have to win. This book will not only help you understand your rela-

tionship with money (*your* Money Why); it will also infuse you with
the confidence and motivation to hopefully reach your financial goals.

Three Things to Remember from This Chapter

1. Mary was a freaking adorable kid.

2. Where you start is not where you finish.

3. When times get tough, make Crystal's chocolate martini:

INGREDIENTS

- 1½ ounces Godiva chocolate liqueur

- 1½ ounces Crème de Cacao

- ½ ounce vanilla vodka

- 2½ ounces half-and-half

- chocolate syrup, for rim

DIRECTIONS

1. Mix all ingredients in a cocktail shaker filled with ice and shake.

2. Pour into a chilled martini glass that is rimmed with chocolate syrup and has a single Hershey's Kiss on the bottom.

CHAPTER 2

THE BIG SIN AND THE BIG LIE

I've always operated under the assumption that audiences
don't always know when they're being lied to, but they
always know when they're being told the truth.

—SEAN PENN

On Labor Day 1974, President Gerald Ford signed the Employee Retirement Income Security Act (ERISA). This 537-page piece of legislation was intended to secure pensions for American workers. Among its many provisions was the requirement that employers insure their plans through the newly created Pension Benefit Guaranty Corporation. It also defined when and how these plans were to be funded.[3]

While the intent was good, ERISA had unforeseen consequences. Someone missed the point that employers were *not required* to have pension plans. They did so to attract employees. At this time almost all plans were employer funded. Workers didn't have to contribute

---

3   "Employee Retirement Income Security Act of 1974," Wikipedia, https://en.wikipedia.org/wiki/Employee_Retirement_Income_Security_Act_of_1974.

anything to secure their retirements. But this legislation significantly increased the cost of those pension plans to employers.

The stage was set for the collapse of the pension system. In my opinion, this was the Big Sin.

In 1975, unemployment reached a post–World War II high of 8.8 percent. By 1982, it was 10.8 percent.[4] In 1980 inflation was at 13.55 percent,[5] and by October 1981 the thirty-year mortgage rate was 18.45 percent.[6]

Unemployment was high, cash was expensive to borrow, and corporate profits were down. Companies didn't have any problem getting workers, and they were looking to cut costs. I had a front-row seat for what happened next. I was working in the finance and accounting department at General Battery. It was my first job, and I loved it. I thought I would work for General Battery for the rest of my life. But its income statement was not looking good. The company was in trouble. With the economy in shambles, no one was buying cars; thus nobody needed batteries. At first, we renegotiated our contracts with suppliers; then we laid people off. Finally—and I remember being in the conference room the day it happened—someone said, "You know, these pensions are costing us a lot of money. We're not required by law to fund them, so why don't we just stop doing that?"

Even though I was participating in General Battery's pension plan (although not fully vested), I thought this was a great solution. It would instantly make the profit and loss (P&L) statement look better. I was young and stupid (and many, many years away from

---

4   "Unemployment Rate by Month for 1975," Federal Reserve Bank of St. Louis, https://fred.stlouisfed.org/graph/?g=wEx7.

5   "US Inflation Rate 1960–2024," Macrotrends, https://www.macrotrends.net/global-metrics/countries/USA/united-states/inflation-rate-cpi.

6   "Contract Rate on 30-Year, Fixed-Rate Conventional Home Mortgage Commitments," Federal Reserve Bank of St. Louis, https://fred.stlouisfed.org/data/MORTG.

retirement), so I supported freezing the pensions. I had no idea what a big deal this was or how harmful the consequences would be to our employees. And I don't think the employees knew either, because I never heard any complaints.

The same thing was happening in boardrooms across America—workers were losing their pensions. But the government had supplied some safety nets. ERISA established the Individual Retirement Account (IRA), which could be opened through a bank or brokerage firm. Contributions were tax deductible, but the onus to save was entirely on the individual.

> This is when the burden for retirement shifted from the employer, the union, and the government to you.

Four years later, Congress passed the Revenue Act of 1978, which made it a bit easier to save. It included a provision—section 401(k)—that created the "employer-sponsored" retirement plan. Companies that chose to offer this benefit would automatically deduct a portion of each paycheck (specified by the employee) and provide options for self-directed investment. These contributions were made with pretax dollars, meaning the money went into your retirement account before it got taxed. An added incentive was that companies could choose to match a portion of your contributions, but few did.[7]

This all sounded fine and dandy at the time. But almost no one knew what this really meant for retirement. In 2013 the Economic Policy Institute would declare the 401(k) a "poor substitute" for the

---

7   "Revenue Act of 1978," Wikipedia, https://en.wikipedia.org/wiki/Revenue_Act_
     of_1978#:~:text=2763%2C%20enacted%20November%206%2C%201978,to%20
     46%20percent)%2C%20increasing%20the.

previous system.[8] That same year, in a *Wall Street Journal* article, Gerald Facciani, former head of the American Society of Pension Professionals & Actuaries, would state that the 401(k) was "oversold."[9]

In my opinion, this was the Big Lie. We were told, "Don't worry. This is easy. You can save for retirement yourself!" Nearly fifty years later, this is the root of our current retirement crisis and the source of the financial angst many are feeling today.

I mean, cut me a break. You're telling me that parents, teachers, plumbers, engineers, and healthcare workers were supposed to figure this out on their own? Corporate pension committees typically rely on financial experts to advise them on investments. Now ordinary people were supposed to do this? It made no sense.

I was also in the room when General Battery pitched the 401(k) to its employees. I didn't sign up, not because I thought it was a bad idea but because I wasn't going to voluntarily reduce my take-home pay. I was a young woman with school loans, car payments, and rent. I couldn't afford that. Millions of Americans across the country were making the same decision. The recession of the early 1980s was still raging. *Nobody* could afford that.

In retrospect, all this really makes me mad. After meeting with hundreds of people in my practice who had their pensions either eliminated or frozen back then, I can tell you that not one understood the gravity of what had happened until they were at or near retirement. And that includes me.

After General Battery, I went to work for Kellogg's. When I left there in 1988, I had accrued a small pension. The company gave

---

8   "Private-Sector Pension Coverage Fell by Half over Two Decades," Economic Policy Institute, https://www.epi.org/blog/private-sector-pension-coverage-decline/.

9   "The Champions of the 401(k) Lament the Revolution They Started," *Wall Street Journal*, https://www.wsj.com/articles/the-champions-of-the-401-k-lament-the-revolution-they-started-1483382348.

me the option of cashing it out or rolling it into an IRA. I was still young and stupid, so I cashed out and bought a beautiful diamond ring. Twenty years later, the ring was stolen. Great decision, huh? To beat myself up, I calculated that my pension would have been worth $170,000 today if I had invested it. Ack!

You've probably heard the saying *caveat emptor*, which is Latin for "buyer beware." It's a principle in contract law that places the responsibility for due diligence on the buyer. This prevents you, the buyer, from going after the seller later—even if the seller had more information than you did at the time of the sale. My niece teaches Latin. I'm going to ask her if there's a phrase that means "let the retiree beware."

So, what started as well-intentioned legislation designed to help secure employee pensions ended up causing the retirement crisis we're facing today (see survey, next page).

After the burden of retirement shifted from the government, companies, and unions to the workers, as if that wasn't bad enough, when the workers had no idea what to do or how to handle this, we yelled at them. *What do you mean you don't understand this?!* As a result, all these years later, almost every person or couple who comes into my office for the first time ends up apologizing. They apologize for not doing a better job with their money. They apologize for not understanding investments better. They apologize for not saving enough, even before we figure out what "enough" is for them. This is a constant, no matter how well they've done! They just "shoulda" all over themselves.

SURVEY SAYS

THE RETIREMENT CRISIS*

% of Americans who worry they'll run out of money if they stop working = **51%**

% of American retirees who wish they'd started saving/ investing earlier = **70%**

From the State of US Financial Capability conducted in 2018 by the FINRA Investor Education Foundation[10] and the 2022 Retiree Reflections Survey conducted by the Employee Benefit Research Institute,[11] respectively

The Memo You Never Got

Consider Betty and Jack. They were in their mid-to-late fifties and excited about retiring at age sixty-two. They came to me to make sure everything was fine and to develop a plan for retirement. I calculated their anticipated annual income and expenses (living costs, healthcare, travel, cars, home maintenance, etc.). They were particularly proud of having saved $720,000. But after I ran the numbers, I realized there

---

10   Judy T. Lin et al., "The State of US Financial Capability: The 2018 National Financial Capability Study," June 2019, https://finrafoundation.org/sites/finrafoundation/files/NFCS-2018-Report-Natl-Findings.pdf.

11   Bridget Bearden, "Retiree Reflections," June 16, 2022, https://www.ebri.org/content/retiree-reflections.

was no way they could retire at sixty-two given what they had in the bank and the lifestyle they desired.

They were shocked. They insisted that $720,000 was a lot of money, and I wholeheartedly agreed. They told me their parents hadn't saved anywhere near that much but had retired at sixty-two and done fine. I pointed out that their parents both received sizable pensions and full healthcare benefits. Betty and Jack had only one small pension and would have to pay for healthcare until they reached Medicare age. Assuming they'd need $100,000 per year to live on, that nest egg would last only seven years. Even if they reduced their annual expenses to $75,000, the money would run out in ten years.

Let me be very clear. Betty and Jack were not stupid people. They had a joint annual income of $175,000. They'd worked hard. They'd been diligent with their spending. They'd saved a sizable amount. But when they realized the reality of their financial situation, they began blaming themselves and, yes, apologizing to me.

Like millions of Americans, Betty and Jack hadn't done anything wrong. It's just that no one ever sent them the memo detailing all the economic changes that had occurred since their parents retired. What do any of us know about retirement? We know what we've experienced. What did we experience? Our parents' retirement. This scenario has played out in my practice many, many times.

Tell me, did anyone ever sit you down and explain the following?

- How much you'd need in your IRA or 401(k) before you could retire?

- How long it might take you to save that much?

- Exactly what an IRA or 401(k) is?

- How an IRA or 401(k) works?

- The percentage of your salary you need to put away to maintain your lifestyle in retirement?

- How much less you'd have to spend to achieve your goal?

Did anyone tell you?

Well, here's the memo you never got:

> This is not your parents' retirement. The burden has shifted to you, the worker. It's almost impossible for someone who isn't in finance to have a handle on all its nuances. So, stop beating yourself up over it. You have absolutely no reason to feel shame and guilt if your retirement nest egg is more like a robin's than an ostrich's. You've been told that this is simple, that you can take care of it yourself, that anyone can understand it. But that's a lie. I don't know how anyone can possibly do this while building a career, raising a family, and/or taking care of parents. People are busy—really busy. It's not that you don't have the smarts to handle this; you just don't have the time and/or interest.

So, relax. Stop apologizing and beating yourself up. We can fix this.

The Pension Dimension

Let's start with understanding what a pension really is and how it works. A pension is a defined benefit program designed to replace a significant portion of your salary after you retire. Traditionally, it was funded entirely by your employer or a union and even extended to your spouse after your death.

How was your pension calculated? In most cases, your average salary for the last five years was multiplied by a factor (often 1.25 percent). The result was then multiplied by the number of years you were enrolled in the plan. Got that? It's similar to Social Security. Earn more, get more. Work longer, get more.

In the wake of the ERISA, these defined *benefit* programs were replaced by defined *contribution* plans, commonly referred to as IRA, 401(k), or 403(b) retirement savings accounts. Although contribution plans had the same goal as benefit plans—replacing a significant portion of your salary after you retire—the onus to amass those funds was now on *you*. Employers could opt to match a portion of your contributions, but they were not obligated to do so.

Here's a quick comparison:

DEFINED BENEFIT PLAN (PENSION)	DEFINED CONTRIBUTION PLAN (401(K))
Employer funded	Employee funded
Actuaries determine the yearly contribution to reach your goal	You determine the yearly contribution to reach your goal
Employer handles investments	You handle investments
Contributions didn't reduce paycheck	Contributions deducted from paycheck
Insured by the Pension Benefit Guaranty Corporation	Gain or loss determined by your investment choices

See the problem with this? While contribution plans were of great benefit to companies, they were a recipe for disaster for workers. A struggling young couple needed not only the wherewithal to sacrifice monthly income to save for retirement but also the savvy to decide where to invest their savings. That's like getting to choose your anesthesia for an operation. Ridiculous.

Plus, back in 1981, with the country in such dire economic straits, it wasn't realistic to expect people to open an IRA or a 401(k). So, that young struggling couple never got into the habit of saving for retirement, and today they're realizing their predicament.

SURVEY *SAYS* — THE RETIREMENT CRISIS*

% of people who were eligible for a 401(k) or 403(b) and did not contribute = **19%**

From a 2024 survey of 212 clients conducted by Evans Wealth Strategies

Here are the three ways saving for retirement played out. (Warning: math alert!)

Fully Funded Pension (Traditional)

- You started at the company at age thirty.

- You worked for thirty-five years and retired at age sixty-five.

- Average salary over the last five years = $100,000.

- Pension is $100,000 x 0.0125 x 35 = $43,750.

- Lifetime benefit if you live to age ninety = $43,750 x 25, or … **$1,093,075.**

Pension Frozen After Fifteen Years (No 401(k))

- You started at the company at age thirty.

- You worked for thirty-five years and retired at age sixty-five.

- Average salary over the last five years = $100,000.

- Pension plan frozen at age forty-five; average salary over the last five years back then = $40,000.

- Pension is $40,000 x 0.0125 x 15 = $7,500.

- Lifetime benefit if you live to age ninety = $7,500 x 25, or … **$187,500**.

Let me shout this from the rooftop: *this is a big deal!* The difference between having a fully funded pension until retirement and a pension that was frozen after fifteen years is $905,575.

Your company's decision to freeze its pension plan meant you needed to save nearly $1 million in your 401(k) to break even. Even I'm sweating. Of course, there's no way you could have known this. I mean, really, not a single employee did. And it wasn't much better for those who opened a 401(k).

Pension Frozen After Fifteen Years (with 401(k))

- You started at the company at age thirty.

- You worked for thirty-five years and retired at age sixty-five.

- Average salary over the last five years = $100,000.

- Pension plan frozen at age forty-five.

- Opened a 401(k) and contributed 5 percent of annual salary each year. (No company match; funds invested in a conservative mutual fund with an assumed rate of return of 7 percent.)

- Average pay raise over the last twenty years = 4.7 percent.

- Lifetime benefit if you live to age ninety = $187,500 from frozen pension + $131,919 in 401(k), or ... **$319,419**.

So, even though you followed the government's advice, opened that 401(k), contributed regularly, and invested conservatively, you're still short $773,656. It's easy to see why so many people are now screaming into retirement without enough funds.

How many people are we talking about? The good news is that some job sectors (teachers, police, military, government ...) still offer fully funded pensions, and their employees can enjoy greater confidence in retirement. But that's the minority. According to JP Morgan, here are the percentages of people currently covered by pensions, by age group:

- Silent generation (ages 79+): 51 percent

- Baby boomers (ages 60–78): 39 percent

- Generation X (ages 44–59): 24 percent

- Millennials (ages 28–43): 16 percent

- Generation Z (ages 23–27): 8 percent[12]

As you can see, this is a big problem. If we educate the millennials and Gen Zers early, they should be okay. But for the boomers and Gen Xers, there's going to be some teeth gnashing. JP Morgan has also calculated the percentage of your income you'll need to save to reach your "income replacement goal," which basically means maintaining the same lifestyle as when you were working. (Keep in mind, this is not an exact science. The numbers will vary based on the return you earn on your investments and how long you live. This model assumes annual household incomes of $100,000, $200,000, and $300,000.)

---

12   "Percentage of Households with a Pension," LIMRA Secure Retirement Institute Analysis of 2019 Survey of Consumer Finances, Federal Reserve Board 2020.

ANNUAL % OF SALARY YOU MUST SAVE IF STARTING NOW WITH NO RETIREMENT SAVINGS[13]

NECESSARY SAVINGS RATE BY HOUSEHOLD INCOME AND AGE

	CURRENT HOUSEHOLD INCOME		
	$100,000	$200,000	$300,000
AGE	SAVINGS RATE (X CURRENT HOUSEHOLD INCOME)		
30	12%	15%	17%
40	20%	27%	31%
50	42%	56%	63%

How to use: Go to the intersection of your closest age and household income. This is your percentage of savings needed. Example: If you're forty with a household income of $200,000, you must start saving 27 percent of your income every year until retirement. This assumes you retire at sixty-five, your spouse is sixty-three, you have thirty-five years in retirement, and your portfolio is diversified among stocks and bonds.

This is not your parents' retirement. We need to start educating ourselves and our kids as fast as we can. We can't go back and change the past, but we can make good decisions now. When is the best time to plant a shade tree? Forty years ago. When is the second-best time? Today!

---

13 *JP Morgan Guide to Retirement 2024*, https://am.jpmorgan.com/content/dam/jpm-am-aem/global/en/insights/retirement-insights/guide-to-retirement-us.pdf.

Saving for Survival

In the wake of all this "glorious" legislation, almost everyone needed financial help, but there wasn't a good system in place to provide it. Stockbrokers mostly wanted to help the super wealthy. Insurance companies sold policies that didn't provide enough for retirement. And financial advisors were largely nonexistent. Indeed, the first class of Certified Financial Planner® professionals (CFP®s) graduated in 1972. There were thirty-five people. The CFP Board, which promotes financial planning services, wasn't even founded until 1985. Today, more than a hundred thousand professionals in the United States hold a CFP® certification.[14] This is good news, but considering that 4.1 million people are expected to retire in 2024, it's not enough.[15]

Back in the 1950s, 1960s, and 1970s, with your employer handling your retirement, if you had some extra money to invest, you did this:

- You called a "stockbroker."

- He (the broker was almost always a he) suggested a stock to buy.

- You bought it. (Good chance it was a car or oil company.)

- You put the stock certificate in a safety-deposit box at the bank.

- The company paid you a quarterly dividend, which you spent on a fancy dinner or something for the house or saved for a vacation.

---

14   "History of the CFP Board," CFP Board, 2024, https://www.cfp.net/about-cfp-board/history#:~:text=In%201972%2C%20IAFP%20enrolled%20its,Planners%20(ICFP)%20in%201973.

15   "A New Chapter in America's Retirement Landscape," Alliance for Lifetime Income, https://www.protectedincome.org/peak65/.

- You passed away.

- Your kids opened the safety-deposit box and found the certificate.

- They were surprised at how much the stock was worth, and now they remember you as a great investor.

Change happens slowly. Many of the people who are in my industry, or are attracted to it, still love selling stocks. That's fine, but clients nowadays need much more. They're not saving for extras; they're saving for survival—and that takes planning.

When many of us were born (certainly the boomers), our responsibility for retirement was very limited. Beyond having our pensions covered, college tuition was affordable, and most people had great health insurance. Plus, people weren't living as long, nor were they managing chronic disease for decades.

My father was a member of the United Auto Workers. He was diagnosed with leukemia at age sixty-four, so he had to retire. My mother was a hardworking, unpaid stay-at-home mom. Pretty typical of those days. The general wisdom at that time was that you were ready for retirement when

- your mortgage was paid off,

- you had a relatively new car,

- your appliances were new (or somewhat new), and

- the kids were out on their own (which used to happen before age thirty).

My parents' retirement went well financially. Unfortunately, Dad passed away within a few years. (Back then, when most people had cancer or heart disease, they didn't have many years left.) Mom lived another twenty-four years. How did she make it work? She received my father's Social Security, his pension, and the union's retiree healthcare.

Having health insurance for the rest of her life was a game changer. When she turned eighty, she was diagnosed with lymphoma. Although doctors gave her a year to live, she survived another eight. Her doctor visits, prescriptions, hospitalizations, dentures, hearing aids … they were all covered. Bless her heart, one day she complained that "they're charging me four dollars for my prescriptions!" I strongly suggested she not complain about this to anyone else. I feared for her safety.

Indeed, for those twenty-four years, Mom had almost zero medical bills. My, how things have changed. Nowadays, people are happy if their out-of-pocket healthcare costs in any given year are less than $5,000.

During my working life, these are the changes I've seen:

- Pensions disappeared or were frozen.

- Lifetime healthcare benefits were eliminated.

- Healthcare costs rose dramatically. (Annual per capita in 1970 = $353; in 2022 = $13,493.)[16]

- Unions have shrunk. (In 1954, 34.7 percent of workers belonged; in 2023, 11.2 percent.)[17]

- Average life expectancy rose. (Sixty-nine years in 1955; seventy-nine years in 2020.)[18]

---

16   "Total National Health Expenditures US $ per Capita 1970–2022," KFF analysis of National Health Expenditure (NHE) data.

17   "Labor Unions in the United States," Wikipedia, https://en.wikipedia.org/wiki/Labor_unions_in_the_United_States#cite_note-27; US Bureau of Labor Statistics, https://www.bls.gov/opub/ted/2024/16-2-million-wage-and-salary-workers-were-represented-by-a-union-in-2023.htm.

18   "US Life Expectancy 1950–2024," Macrotrends, https://www.macrotrends.net/global-metrics/countries/USA/united-states/life-expectancy.

- Long-term healthcare insurance became a necessity. (Seventy percent of people are expected to need it, and they'll use it for three years.)[19]

- Long-term healthcare costs increased dramatically. (In the last year or two, premiums have almost doubled.)[20]

- The government made promises it couldn't keep. (Social Security and Medicare are both underfunded.)

This is a ton of financial change in one lifetime. Too much for anyone to deal with on their own. You need expert guidance. The problem is, many of today's experts are entertainers rather than educators …

Three Things to Remember from This Chapter

1. The Big Sin is that the burden for retirement shifted from employers, the government, or the union to you.

2. The Big Lie is that they told you it was so easy you could do it yourself.

3. This is not your fault.

---

19 "The Need for Long-Term Care Continues to Grow," Pennsylvania Health Care Organization, https://www.phca.org/for-consumers/research-data/long-term-and-post-acute-care-trends-and-statistics/.

20 "Long-Term Care Insurance Rate Increases and Reduced Benefit Options," Center for Insurance Policy and Research, https://content.naic.org/sites/default/files/long-term-care-insurance-rate-increases-and-reduced-benefit-options-insights-from-interviews-with-financial-planners.pdf.

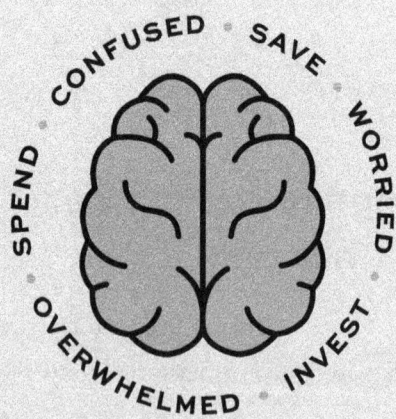

CHAPTER 3

IGNORE THE "EXPERTS"

You cannot shame or belittle people into changing their behaviors.
—BRENÉ BROWN

What is it about money that makes people yell? You turn on CNBC, and they're yelling. You spend too much money, or just some money, and your partner or parent yells at you. Why? Because money is freaking emotional! It's something we must deal with every single day, and yet we have a really hard time having reasonable conversations about it.

By the way, if you yell, "MARY, DON'T EAT THE CHOCOLATE CAKE!" oh, I'm gonna eat the chocolate cake. I'm not a Navy SEAL. I hear that yelling works on them. (I guess that's why there are so few Navy SEALs.)

A lot of people don't seek financial help because they're afraid of being yelled at. For some crazy reason, financial planning is an area of life where we think yelling is a good idea. Yet we know from studies that being shamed or yelled at doesn't lead people to change their behavior (at least not permanently).

For example, University of British Columbia researchers examined the effects of shame on recovering alcoholics. Public shaming has traditionally been viewed as a way to encourage people to amend their ways, so they set out to see if that's true. Study participants recruited from Alcoholics Anonymous completed questionnaires about their physical and mental health. Their answers provided the first evidence that feeling shame about one's addiction can directly promote relapses. "Our research suggests that shaming people for difficult-to-curb behaviors may be exactly the wrong approach to take," concluded the study authors. "Rather than prevent future occurrences of such behaviors, shaming may lead to an increase in these behaviors."[21]

Granted, alcoholism and poor financial decision-making are two entirely different animals, but I believe there's a correlation. Author and researcher Brené Brown calls shame a silent epidemic because people don't want to talk about it. We prefer to pretend it's not happening to us. But ironically, we enjoy watching other people get shamed. In fact, shaming has become a popular form of entertainment. TV shows and podcasts that feature hostile confrontations are consistently top rated. But Brown's research shows that the by-products of shame and blame are fear and disconnection.[22]

After starting my business, I realized I needed to let my clients know they were in a no-shame, no-blame zone. But how could I do this quickly and effectively? My go-to has always been humor. So, after they finished apologizing for what they did or didn't do or for what they knew or didn't know, I'd tell them if they wanted to be judged,

---

21 Daniel Randles and Jessica L. Tracy, "Nonverbal Displays of Shame Predict Relapse and Declining Health in Recovering Alcoholics," *Clinical Psychological Science* (2013): https://doi.org/10.1177/2167702612470645.

22 Brené Brown, "On Shame and Accountability," *Unlocking Us*, July 1, 2020, https://brenebrown.com/podcast/brene-on-shame-and-accountability/.

then I'd have to charge extra because (a) I didn't want to judge them, and (b) it's a lot more work.

But even that didn't stop their apologizing. Next, they'd apologize for not knowing more about what I do and the services I provide, which is crazy. I'd ask them what they do for a living. It didn't really matter what their answer was—I'd accurately point out that I couldn't go to their place of work and do their job, so why should they expect to know how to do mine? I especially love talking to healthcare workers. I tell them that if I had to do their job—even for a single hour—people would die. I'm not kidding. I faint at the sight of blood. When I was dating my current husband, who worked in the operating room, I insisted on no shoptalk at home.

Education or Entertainment?

So, people are blaming themselves for just about everything, and they're desperate for financial help. But because of all this shaming and blaming, they aren't seeking the help they need. Rather than make an appointment with a Certified Financial Planner® professional and drag their worried butts into the office for a conversation they dread, they're turning to TV personalities, podcasters, and social media influencers instead. And what do they get? *More* shame and blame.

I think you can see the problem here. Even though they aren't getting shamed in person, if they're in a financial situation similar to what's being discussed (no retirement savings, high credit card debt …), the effect is the same. It may feel less painful, but they're going to hold that shame inside either way. Sometimes, the most pain is self-inflicted.

The other day I happened across a financial radio show while driving home from work. The caller was a young, intelligent woman who was trying to get out from under a crushing amount of debt that she and her husband had accumulated. The host asked if she'd completely lost her mind; then, he berated her for getting into such a situation and told her she deserved to be scared.

This really upset me. Professional financial advisors would never respond this way. But hosts like this can get away with it because the people they're advising won't show up in their office the following week. They don't have the day-to-day responsibility for their financial success. There's no accountability. It's strictly entertainment.

Other financial celebrities prefer lecturing to yelling. They speak in slow, well-enunciated diction that makes me feel like English is my second language. One podcast I listened to recently opened with the host chastising the audience about emailing incorrectly. The host then went on to say that when it comes to saving for retirement, the listeners are still getting it "so, so, so wrong" and that today the show would take them back to school.

I did feel like I was back in school—but it was grade school, I'd glued Blaire's ponytail to the back of her chair, and I was sitting in the principal's office awaiting punishment.

The king of yelling, however, is on CNBC. Jim Cramer's rants are epic, and his show *Mad Money* features more shouting than a Liverpool-versus-Manchester United soccer match. Every time I tune in, I'm half expecting him to drop dead of a heart attack. (By the way, I never ring a bell when I make a stock purchase or shout, "Booyah!") In an interview with Jon Stewart in 2009, Cramer said this: "I'm not Eric Sevareid. I'm not Edward R. Murrow. I'm a guy trying to do an entertainment show about business for people to watch."[23]

---

23   "On Daily Show, Stewart, Cramer Get Serious," NPR, March 13, 2009, https://www.npr.org/transcripts/101888064.

I'd like to believe that people watch him primarily for entertainment, not financial advice, but I'm not so sure about that.

These are just a few examples. I could go on and on. No matter who it is, there's always some degree of yelling and an undercurrent of accusations such as "You're dumb" or "You don't know what you're doing." If you watch or listen long enough, you start to believe that, and it gradually beats you down.

Maybe even a bigger problem than blame is the fact that they don't know you. They don't have the whole picture. It's like a doctor giving you a diagnosis without knowing your medical history and vitals. You may get some quick answers to a general question, but this is not the advice you need to meet your goals.

No wonder everyone's apologizing.

Even worse, since there's no filter or fact-checking on social media, some influencers are supplying financial information or advice that's misleading or just plain wrong. In 2022 Kim Kardashian agreed to pay $1.26 million to the Securities and Exchange Commission (SEC) to settle a charge of unlawfully promoting EthereumMax, a crypto asset security, on her Instagram account. Her original post had included a link to a website, which provided instructions for buying the tokens. Kardashian did not disclose she was being paid for the promotion.

"This case is a reminder that, when celebrities or influencers endorse investment opportunities, including crypto asset securities, it doesn't mean that those investment products are right for all investors," said SEC chair Gary Gensler.[24]

---

24   "SEC Charges Kim Kardashian for Unlawfully Touring Crypto Security," US Securities and Exchange Commission press release, https://www.sec.gov/newsroom/press-releases/2022-183#:~:text=%22Investors%20are%20entitled%20to%20know,of%20a%20celebrity%20or%20influencer.

The number of fans who took Kardashian's advice and lost money in the volatile crypto market is unknown. But given how many women are getting Botox and butt lifts, I'm guessing it was quite a few.

MoneySuperMarket.com recently analyzed 350 videos from so-called "finfluencers" (financial influencers) on social media and found that 74 percent contained "poor, misleading, high risk, or potentially harmful" advice.[25] Another recent report, this one from the Chartered Financial Analyst Institute, uncovered that only 20 percent of all financial influencers on TikTok, Instagram, and YouTube disclosed their professional status and whether they were compensated for recommending certain products.[26]

The difference between these finfluencers and a Certified Financial Planner® professional like me is that finfluencers are salespeople. Whether they're pushing a specific financial product or their personal brand, your connection with them is purely transactional. You're a follower, a listener, and maybe even a buyer of whatever it is they're promoting. Even though it may feel like you have a relationship with them, you don't. As the tone of some of their posts and podcasts suggest, they don't really care about you.

25 Meg Bratley, "74% of Influencer 'Finance Hack' Videos Contain Dangerous, Misleading, Incorrect or 'Nonsense' Advice," *IFA Magazine*, June 2, 2024, https://ifamagazine.com/74-of-influencer-finance-hack-videos-contain-dangerous-misleading-incorrect-or-nonsense-advice/.

26 "How TikTok Is Transforming Financial Advice," CFA Institute, https://www.cfainstitute.org/en/professional-insights-stories/how-tiktok-transforming-financial-advice#:~:text=In%20the%20analysis%20by%20CFA,influencers%20before%20trusting%20their%20advice.

SURVEY *SAYS*

OUTCOME OF TAKING FINANCIAL ADVICE FROM TV, SOCIAL MEDIA, OR PODCAST*

Good = **14%** | Bad = **9%** | So-so = **77%**

From a 2024 survey of 212 clients conducted by Evans Wealth Strategies

I, on the other hand, must field your phone calls during market downturns, answer your emails when a family crisis occurs, and sit with you in my office for annual reviews. We have an actual relationship, and it's often complicated by emotions, biases, and all the baggage from these other sources. This impedes people's ability to make good financial decisions, because they can't think clearly when they feel blame, shame, guilt, and inadequacy. People are most vulnerable and will agree to anything when they're being yelled at.

That's why my office and this book are safe zones. Instead of numbing you with charts and graphs or trying to sell you something that just benefits me, I prefer getting to your core emotions about money—your Money Why. This involves encouraging you to share your vulnerabilities while also sharing mine. It involves empathy, respect, and trust. And in the end, it's magic. After all, I'm not really the expert; you are. No one knows you better than you. My job is to simply open your eyes to who you are financially.

People's greatest desire is not to be loved but to be understood. You're not alone. There is no stigma or shame if you're fifty-five and your 401(k) is underfunded, or if you don't even know what a 401(k) is. Don't stand for being labeled as an "unsuccessful" investor by the financial "experts."

Who Should You Be Talking To?

I'm not saying that every traditional financial advisor is good and trustworthy and beyond this type of criticism. They are not. But there are baseline credentials to look for.

When you see a doctor, you know that they went to college, attended medical school, and did an internship and residency. It's a grueling process. My brother, who's two years older than me, is a doctor. I witnessed everything he went through to become an MD. He's the smart one in the family. We never play trivia against him.

Teachers are similar. To be hired, they need to meet certain qualifications and complete ongoing training. So do airline pilots, truck drivers, and nurses. It's all very reassuring, but what I also admire about these people is that they love learning. That's important. Before I hire someone, I make sure they love learning. Even though I've been in the financial field for forty-five years, I come across something new almost every week. That's one of the things I enjoy about this profession: boredom is a stranger.

So why do people spend more time finding a good mechanic or plumber than they do a financial advisor? One reason: the average investor has no idea what the various financial advising titles mean, let alone the requirements for obtaining them.

The Financial Industry Regulatory Authority (FINRA), whose job is protecting American investors, lists 253 financial designations. Yikes! These range from Bucket Plan Certified to Registered Financial Gerontologist to Rollover Specialist. (I had a dog who could have qualified for the latter.) Ironically, FINRA has no official designations for "financial advisor" and "financial planner."[27]

Although the titles *financial advisor* and *financial planner* sound authoritative, the truth is that there are no formal qualifications you must meet to use those titles. Some states require a high school diploma and passing a simple test, but many don't. Comparatively, a CFP® professional has a college degree, at least three years of experience, has taken eight master-level-type courses, and passed a grueling test.[28] Being certified or not certified is extremely different. Are you talking to a cardiologist or a gynecologist? It's pretty important.

In other words, all financial designations are not created equal. Some have rigorous standards that must be met and maintained to keep that title. Some encourage investors to verify the status of anyone claiming to hold that title. And some have a formal disciplinary process to handle grievances. Other designations are relatively easy to earn and can be maintained by simply paying a yearly fee. And just because a certain title requires an official FINRA examination doesn't mean its holder is the financial equivalent of a brain surgeon.

You can find out what it takes to earn and maintain a financial designation by using FINRA's Professional Designations Database. Keep in mind that while designations often imply a degree of special training or experience, they can also be tools for marketing or self-promotion. Be wary of anyone who makes too much of their title and tries to tout it as the reason you should hire them. A professional designation should never be the sole reason you select an investment professional.

---

27   FINRA Professional Designations Database, https://www.finra.org/investors/professional-designations.

28   "The Certification Process," CFP Board, https://www.cfp.net/get-certified/certification-process.

Don't feel bad if you didn't know any of this. No one does. When I first met my husband, he told me he was a CRNA. I didn't know what a CRNA was, but I didn't want to appear dumb by asking him. On our third date, I inquired how he liked being a CNA. He looked at me like I was crazy. I was puzzled. *What did I do?* He emphatically said he wasn't a CNA; he was a CRNA!

I soon learned that a CNA is a certified nursing assistant. You must be sixteen years old, complete a four-week course, and pass a state test. A CRNA is a certified registered nurse anesthetist. It takes about seven or eight years of education and experience, including a college degree and three years of anesthetist school.

"Oh, I get it!" I said. He was kind, and I apologized. But frankly, I'm shocked we had a fourth date. Medicine wasn't my field, and if finance isn't yours, how would you know the differences between a CFP® and other professional designations?

Unfortunately, as wonderful as it is that the CFP® has been created and that it's starting to incorporate behavioral finance in its educational efforts, the financial industry as a whole is still not addressing the fact that people act on emotion. In the next chapter, I'll prove that.

Three Things to Remember from This Chapter

1. Shaming and yelling only work with Navy SEALs.

2. The most famous financial advisors are primarily entertainers.

3. Although the titles *financial advisor* and *financial planner* sound authoritative, there's no national requirement for calling yourself that.

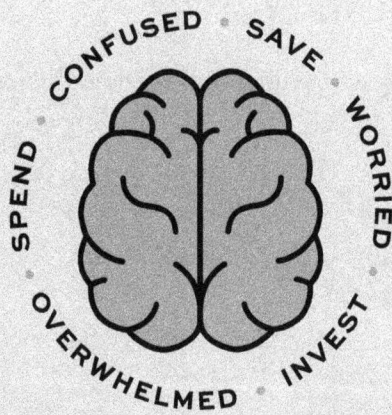

CHAPTER 4

MONEY IS ...

The happiness of your life depends upon the quality of your thoughts.
—MARCUS AURELIUS

You often hear the phrase "He's no good with money." What that really means is that a person has emotions around money that make it difficult for him to make smart financial decisions. If he doesn't address those emotions, he'll never be able to realize his financial goals.

Here's a little exercise I do at my seminars. I ask everyone in the audience to complete this sentence. Don't give it a lot of time or thought; just complete the following sentence: Money is ___.

Here are the most common answers I get:

- Scary

- Scarce

- Security

- Love

- Power

- Confusing

- Overwhelming

- Private

- Hard to get

- Personal

- The root of all evil

- Not my friend!

I've given this quiz to all types of people, and the answers are always the same. No one ever says, "Money is the means for the exchange of goods and services," which is its actual definition. Instead, they define it by the feelings they have toward it. This proves that money is emotional. So while the adage "Money can't buy happiness" is true, your relationship with money can be a happy (or unhappy) one.

You won't make any significant financial progress, however, until you understand your emotional relationship with money, or your Money Why. This will explain why you do the things you do financially.

Rather than telling you what financial decisions you need to make, I'm going to help you identify why you're not already making them. That's a big difference. It's the same with weight loss. It's not enough to be told you need to drop some pounds; you must identify your relationship with food—in other words, why you're not losing weight. The problem isn't what you're eating; it's why you're eating it. Likewise, the problem isn't what you're buying; it's why you're buying it. To achieve Financial Happiness, you must get to the why.

Previous chapters dealt with the big economic issues that impacted you. Now I'm going to delve into the personal issues that impact you, namely your physiology (nature) and your upbringing (nurture).

Nature: How Your Amygdala Gets Hijacked

Could something as small as an almond be driving your decisions? It sure can. Meet your amygdala. It's one of the oldest parts of the brain. Much older than the prefrontal cortex, which is the reasoning, planning, and decision-making part of the brain. The amygdala is where our primitive fight-or-flight response resides.

The fight-or-flight response is very useful. In fact, your amygdala is why you're alive today. If your ancestors hadn't had one, they'd have been squashed by a woolly mammoth. When a mammoth is stampeding toward you, you don't have time to think. You just need to react (i.e., run like crazy!). The amygdala kicks in automatically, and all the physiological reactions that follow (adrenaline rush, increased heart rate, redirected blood flow ...) are designed to help you survive.

I looked into the eyes of a woolly mammoth in 2009, a year after starting my business. Early one morning, I unlocked the door and was standing in the lobby (which actually doubled as Crystal's office) when my amygdala kicked in. My heart started racing, my palms got sweaty, and I couldn't catch my breath. I felt like my whole body was vibrating. My only thoughts were *What have I done? Why did I start this business? Why did I risk my financial security? Everyone is going to see what a failure I am and how foolish I've been.* These thoughts kept looping through my mind as if on the Indy racetrack.

Where did these sudden worries come from? What was the trigger? I certainly understood the risks of starting a business. I had spent countless hours running the numbers. But it had been a year, and I hadn't been able to take a dime out of the business. I was working seven days a week, and the economy was tanking. Do you remember 2009? It was the deepest economic downturn since the Great Depression. The S&P 500 dropped 48 percent over a six-month period,[29] unemployment was 9.9 percent,[30] and America's gross domestic product was *negative* 4.3 percent.[31] People were being thrown out of their houses, and here I was holding the keys to a new financial business. *What the heck was I thinking?*

Even though the reasoning part of my brain (the prefrontal cortex) understood the logic of the situation, my amygdala saw it as a woolly mammoth. My clients (the few I had) were scared, demanding empathy as well as answers. Plus, I was exhausted. My amygdala had gotten hijacked.

The term *amygdala hijack* was coined by Daniel Goleman in his book *Emotional Intelligence.* The fight-or-flight response can be triggered by stress, fear, anxiety, jealousy, and anger. These are emotions I see every day in my practice. People are not making financial decisions based on logic; they are making them based on emotion.

SURVEY SAYS

DO YOU BELIEVE EMOTIONS IMPACT YOUR FINANCIAL DECISIONS?*

Yes = **74%** | No = **26%**

From a 2024 survey of 212 clients conducted by Evans Wealth Strategies

---

29 "Stock Prices in Financial Crisis," Federal Reserve Bank of Atlanta, https://www. atlantafed.org/cenfis/publications/notesfromthevault/0909#:~:text=Much%20 of%20the%20decline%20in,low%20on%20March%209%2C%202009.

30 "Historical US Unemployment Rate by Year," Investopedia, https://www.investopedia. com/historical-us-unemployment-rate-by-year-7495494.

31 "The Great Recession," Federal Reserve History, https://www.federalreservehistory. org/essays/great-recession-of-200709#:~:text=Real%20gross%20domestic%20 product%20(GDP,10%20percent%20in%20October%202009.

While the amygdala is best known for sending distress signals that trigger the release of adrenaline, it's also involved in reward processing and releasing dopamine, the feel-good hormone. I recently got to see this up close. I was on vacation with a good friend and client. Her world revolved around how things looked—beautiful design, color, styling ... I always joke that she and I have no overlapping skill sets. Thus, she helps me with colors, and I help her with finances. We'd been working hard to get her finances in order and were making good progress. I was so proud of her. While on vacation she wanted to visit this store that advertised eclectic furniture. Not my thing, but okay, maybe they had free chocolate.

> Me: Do you need any furniture?
> Her: No.
> Me: Then why are we in here?
> Her: I just like to look.
> Me: But if you don't need anything, why look?
> Her: Because it's fun. Oh, Mary, you just don't get it.
> Me: You're right.

After a few minutes (which seemed like an eternity to me because there wasn't any free chocolate), she spotted a full-length hand-carved mirror. It was beautiful, one of a kind, and *very* expensive. I saw her whole demeanor change. Her breathing quickened, her eyes widened, and she spoke excitedly about how wonderful it would look in her home. I knew purchases like this weren't in her financial plan. But I also knew that you can't tell someone who's all excited about a purchase not to go through with it. I also wanted to remain her friend. So, I agreed that it was beautiful and suggested she think about it overnight and come back tomorrow if she still wanted it. It took some persuading, but she finally agreed. The next day after breakfast, I asked if she wanted to get the mirror. She looked at me and said, "Nah, I'm over it."

What happened? The previous day, when she saw the mirror, her amygdala was hijacked. *Buy the mirror! Buy the mirror! It will look great in the hall, and everyone who sees it will know what fabulous taste you have!* But overnight, the amygdala settled down, her level of dopamine subsided, the prefrontal cortex took over, and she realized she didn't really need the mirror—nor could she afford it.

Think of these two parts of the brain, which are wired together, as the "feeling brain" and the "thinking brain." Emotional self-regulation happens when the thinking brain corrects the feeling brain. The amygdala will activate when the threat or reward seems immediate and significant. If the threat or reward seems mild, it can be easily overridden. Different people assess threat and reward differently. One person may fear what people will think of them if they drive an old car or live in a small house. Another may be afraid of not having a safety net of cash in the bank. Neither of these is right or wrong. They're just different.

Whether it was Marcus Aurelius nearly two thousand years ago or Daniel Goleman thirty years ago, theirs is the same message. Your ability to keep your feeling brain from overreacting will determine the life you have.

And there is neuroscience to support this. According to Baba Shiv, a neuroeconomics researcher at Stanford University's Graduate School of Business, the rational brain is only responsible for about 5 percent to 10 percent of our decision-making. "Emotions … have a profound influence on our decisions, and we aren't aware of it," he says.[32]

---

32   "More Than a Feeling: The Keys to Making the Right Choice," *Stanford Business*, March 20, 2024, https://www.gsb.stanford.edu/insights/more-feeling-keys-making-right-choice.

Nurture: Yet Another Way Your Folks Screwed You Up

I love the expression "Genetics loads the gun, but the environment [and your experiences] pull the trigger." My mom was frugal, or as she liked to say, "good with money." One Christmas, I bought her six rolls of aluminum foil so she would stop reusing it. I thought it was hilarious; she didn't. However, I now realize her penny-pinching was also a bit nuts. This intelligent, well-read woman couldn't bring herself to talk about money.

At age eighty, after she was diagnosed with lymphoma and started chemo, she became too weak to handle her finances. She asked if I'd do it for her. I assumed this meant for the rest of her life, but to my surprise, after about a year she got stronger and asked for her checkbook back. I thought she'd be impressed with how well I'd organized everything and what a great job I'd done. Instead, she looked at me and said, "Don't you feel awfully uncomfortable handling someone else's money?"

My inside voice was screaming. *What? Do you know what I do for a living?* Proctologist? No, that's not uncomfortable. But balancing someone's checkbook? Now *that's* uncomfortable. I quickly realized she wasn't questioning my competence. It was my knowing the deep, dark secrets of her financial life (of which there weren't any) that bothered her. She actually made me swear not to divulge anything to my siblings.

Okay, I should have had the guts to ask *why* she'd sworn me to secrecy. True, there wasn't a lot of money. My siblings were all well off. No one had hit Mom up for a loan. Maybe there was a skeleton in a safe deposit box somewhere? But no, even after her death, none ever appeared. Mom was just extremely private about money and Depression-era tight.

Over the years, I've had the privilege of talking to hundreds of families. Let me tell you, people really don't like discussing money. They love bragging about how much money they saved: "I got this car for a great price." "We had a coupon for a two-for-one dinner." Or "I bought this dress at Nordstrom Rack for 80 percent off." But most won't share their income or savings account balances.

If you're like most people, you learned about money from your parents. When I say "money," I mean all aspects of it—incomes, expenses, savings, and investments. Growing up, the only thing I ever heard was how expensive everything was and why I shouldn't waste money. When I was in my early twenties, I gave my dad a birthday card that read:

1. No, I didn't know what I was doing.

2. Yes, I did think money grew on trees.

3. Yes, I did think we owned stock in the electric company.

He loved it.

Where did you learn about money, and what did you learn? Here are some questions I want you to ask yourself:

- Was money discussed in your house when you were growing up?
  - What was said about it?
  - Were these conversations happy or stressful?
- Did your parents ever fight about money?

- Did one person make most of the spending and saving decisions?
  - Was it the wage earner?
- Were financial decisions made by both parents?
- How did the financial discussions you heard educate you?
  - Did you learn only about not wasting money?
  - Did you learn about saving for retirement?
  - Did you learn about stocks and bonds?
  - Was having a financial plan ever mentioned?
  - Did you learn the value of a pension?
  - Did you learn how your wages impact your Social Security benefit?
  - Did you learn the value of having an IRA or 401(k)?
- How is money discussed in your home now?
  - Does one person make most of the spending and saving decisions?
  - Is it the wage earner?
- Do you have money discussions together and agree upon the decisions?
- Do you dread having to discuss money?
- Do you or your partner often hide spending from each other?
- Did you see one of your parents hide spending?

There are no right or wrong answers to these questions. It's simply a way to gain insight into how your Money Why developed. Chances are, you're the way you are because of what you experienced and the examples your parents set.

When a couple comes in to see me, I ask who handles the money. The answer is always the person who pays the bills. They're vaguer when it comes to who handles the investments. In many cases, there isn't one person in charge. For working clients, one may contribute to a 401(k) while the other has a pension plan or no retirement account at all. Either way, they usually think they have it covered.

Of course, they don't discuss their financial future. They probably were never taught about these things, and until they get close to retirement, it's just a faraway goal. They're busy working, raising a family, paying the mortgage, caregiving … It's not right in front of them. But a *big* part of this nonconversation is that, deep down, they really don't want to talk about it. It's uncomfortable, they doubt they're doing the right thing, and they feel guilty. If they were super confident, they would be bragging about it. This level of discomfort extends to talking to family and friends and even a financial advisor.

There are three big life events that bring the investment topic to the forefront:

1. They want to retire, and they want to know if they have enough money.

2. They see their parents struggling financially in retirement.

3. There's a healthcare crisis.

The sad thing is, these events often happen at the eleventh hour, and now the hill is steep. Even worse, some people come to me *after* they've retired. When I ask why they waited so long, they say they didn't really think about it; they thought things would be fine. But I know the *real* reason. They didn't want to talk about it. They didn't want to risk any bad news.

We must start talking about money! I don't mean get-rich schemes or hot stock tips. I mean serious, thoughtful financial planning—educating and helping people reach their long-term financial goals without shame, blame, or judgment. And for God's sake, no yelling.

Some good news: Many of my clients who are near or in retirement are having their children come see me. These are great parents. They don't want their kids to go through what they did. They want them to get the big picture early. When this first started happening, I thought everyone in the family would have similar Money Whys, but I was wrong. Sometimes they did, but most times they were quite different. After getting to know them better, I realized they'd had similar experiences around money while growing up, but they interpreted them in different ways.

Let's say Mom and Dad fought over money. One child might have been horrified and vowed to never have those kinds of arguments with their partner. This results in open and honest financial discussions. Another child from the same family would remember those fights and conclude they weren't so bad since Mom and Dad are still together. *If I fight about money with my spouse, so what? It's part of being married.* But here's the complicating factor: there are two people in the relationship. The examples and experiences that your spouse had growing up change the dynamic.

SURVEY *SAYS* IN YOUR EARLY YEARS, WHO TAUGHT YOU ABOUT MONEY?*

Parents and grandparents = **82%**

WHAT DO YOU REMEMBER MOST ABOUT YOUR PARENTS' MONEY DISCUSSIONS?*

Never heard them talk about money = **45%**

Seemed to be on the same page = **35%**

There were arguments = **19%**

*From a 2024 survey of 212 clients conducted by
Evans Wealth Strategies*

The Trap of Learned Helplessness

In the late 1960s, psychologist Martin Seligman started researching how "learned helplessness" develops in animals and human beings. When someone feels a lack of control over the events in their environment, this undermines their motivation to make changes and alter the situation. The hallmark signs of learned helplessness are:

1. *Personal:* "I am stupid" as opposed to "I did a stupid thing."

2. *Permanent:* "This is never going to get any better" as opposed to "This will pass."

3. *Pervasive:* "I can't do anything right" as opposed to "I'm not very good at this."[33]

So how can this mindset affect your finances? Here are two examples:

---

33 "Learned Helplessness," Wikipedia, https://en.wikipedia.org/wiki/Learned_helplessness.

SCENARIO 1

- You decide to save for retirement (a very good thing).

- You purchase a stock in an account you established.

- You purchase only one stock; you don't diversify, but you've heard good things about it.

- Three months later, the stock drops 30 percent.

- You're scared, angry, and devastated; you sell it at a loss.

- You beat yourself up. You call yourself stupid. Investing is rigged; you'll never do it again.

- You calm down, decide you need help, and call in to a financial radio show.

- The host yells at you for selling and for not saving more.

- Now you really know you're stupid. Investing isn't for you. You never try again. You're done.

- You experience learned helplessness.

- You never accumulate enough money to comfortably retire.

SCENARIO 2

- You decide to save for retirement (a very good thing).

- You purchase only one stock; you don't diversify, but you've heard good things about it.

- Three months later, the stock drops 30 percent.

- You're scared, angry, and devastated; you sell it at a loss.

- You beat yourself up. You call yourself stupid. Investing is rigged; you'll never do it again.

- You calm down, decide you need help, and go see a CFP® professional with an IQ and a heart.

- She compliments you for wanting to plan for retirement.

- She explains how markets work—when, how often, and how much they go up and down. She stops you from beating yourself up. She explains that unless you work in the financial industry, it's very doubtful you'll ever understand everything.

- She explains how investing on your own can be very stressful.

- She teaches you about diversification.

- She takes the time to develop a retirement plan.

- You review and revise your plan with her on a regular basis.

- You look forward to retirement with greater confidence.

Learned helplessness is a common human condition, and when it's applied to a subject like money that is so emotional and confusing, it can mean disaster.

Optimism is almost always a necessary foundation for building wealth. Why start a business or buy stocks if you don't think the future will be better than today? When I started my business, I was optimistic, but staying optimistic can be a struggle.

Can Money Buy Happiness?

The short answer is no. But my joke used to be "Give me the money, and I'll do my own darn shopping." Although money can't buy happiness, it sure can buy options.

People think that anyone who has a lot of money has it made. But that's not the case. A recent article in *Yahoo!Finance UK* written by Danielle McAdam provides a great example of this.[34] Mike Tyson was one of the greatest boxers ever. At age twenty, in 1986, he was the youngest person to ever win the heavyweight title. The next year he signed a $27 million contract with HBO for eight fights. In 1990 he got a Showtime contract for $120 million. In all, it's estimated he earned $430 million from fights and endorsement deals. In 1992 he was sentenced to three years in prison for being a sex offender. In 2003, he filed for bankruptcy.

Think about what it takes to be the heavyweight champion of the world. The discipline he had to have. Getting out of bed and working out when he didn't want to, when he didn't feel good, when no one believed in him. The drive. The ambition. What he didn't understand was money and the emotions surrounding it. He bought a $2.2 million gold-plated tub for his wife, Robin Givens, in 1988. His amygdala or feeling brain was in complete control. Using his celebrity, he has since accumulated a nest egg estimated at around $10 million. Interestingly, he doesn't plan on leaving any inheritance to his kids. He says it would prevent them from overcoming adversity, fending for themselves, and working hard. Mike is not alone here. I've met many wealthy people who feel the same way.

I think Tyson is on to something. I've noticed that the relationship with money is very different if you own it versus inherit it. Of course, this isn't always the case. Some kids really respect the money

34 Danielle McAdam, "How the 'Baddest Man on the Planet' Blew His Huge Fortune," *Yahoo!Finance*, June 26, 2024, https://uk.finance.yahoo.com/news/mike-tyson-blew-millions-161300158.html?guccounter=1&guce_referrer=aHR0cHM6Ly93d3cuZ29vZ2xlLmNvbS88&guce_referrer_sig=AQAAAGp9KIiIyIQ3INTTRqt1_FvK414Oi_wv8R-SA3SEUSoBpGKffrN3qeM_pM675zSSEzwckIEhETl3sX1o0VFhc7pbsROtdF2hEs-Mu1l6w_vCDPqxK1LgpBKRHkbC1oVNRYNUtt0IggWRgI1RISI6CnJjC1ZB_DIqWKzI-UnpL_ztwZX.

their parents worked so hard to earn. But many can't wait to buy a new house, a car, a boat, or a vacation.

Do lottery winners achieve Financial Happiness? There is a lot of research on this—who buys tickets and why, what happens to the money after they win, what amount increases happiness. University of Pennsylvania and Princeton researchers recently found that among the least happy group of study participants, happiness rose with income until $100,000 but then showed no further rise as income continued to grow.[35] Make of that what you will. I'll be happy when ... my circumstances change? No, it's when your *thinking* changes.

What is Financial Happiness, anyway? Being rich? When are you rich? There's a ton of evidence that your perception of *rich* is primarily derived from the people you spend the most time with. If your family and friends seem to have more money than you, you're not rich. If your family and friends seem to have less money than you, you think you're rich.

> My definition of Financial Happiness is having enough money to purchase the things that create pleasure today while knowing that your financial future is safe.

For many of my clients, optimism is not just the key to financial success; it is the key to happiness. The catch-22 is, you don't need optimism to amass enough money for retirement, but without it you'll never feel happy about where you're at.

Now let's figure out *your* Money Why.

---

35   Michele W. Berger, "Does More Money Correlate with Greater Happiness?" *Penn Today*, March 6, 2023, https://penntoday.upenn.edu/news/does-more-money-correlate-greater-happiness-Penn-Princeton-research.

Three Things to Remember
from This Chapter

1. Money is emotional for everyone.

2. Your brain can be hijacked into making foolish choices.

3. Financial Happiness is having enough money to purchase the things that create pleasure today while knowing that your financial future is safe.

PART II
THE EMOTIONS

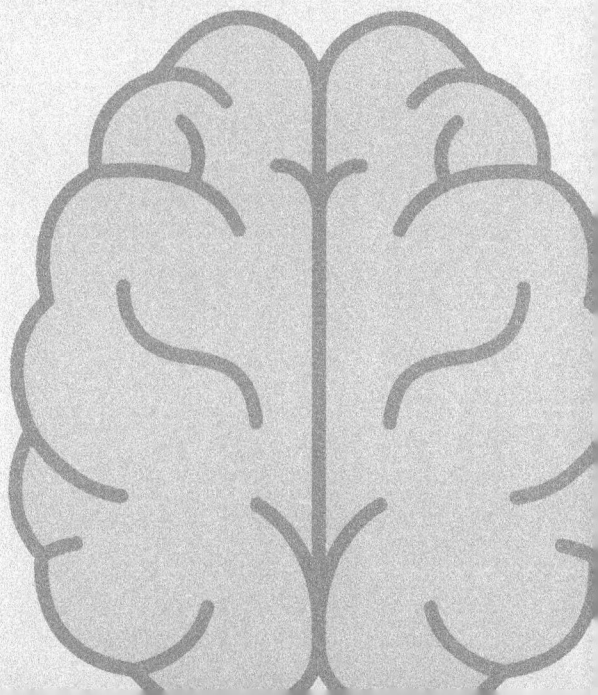

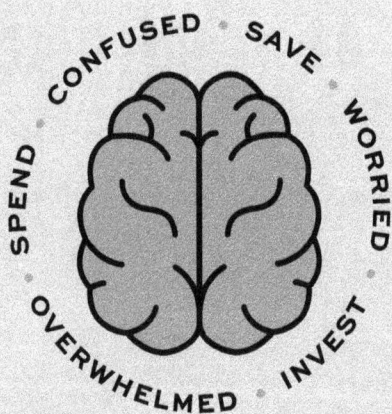

SPEND · CONFUSED · SAVE · WORRIED · INVEST · OVERWHELMED ·

CHAPTER 5

FOMO OR FORO? YOUR MONEY WHY

Money isn't the most important thing in life. But it's reasonably close to oxygen on the gotta-have-it scale.

—ZIG ZIGLAR

This is the most important chapter in the book. You're about to discover your financial personality, or as I like to call it, your Money Why. There are two basic Money Whys: fear of missing out (FOMO) and fear of running out (FORO). Just as your personality (introvert, extrovert) impacts how you interact with the world, your financial personality (FOMO or FORO) influences how you interact with money—how you think about it and behave toward it. It's the why behind every financial decision you make, and very few people have any idea what theirs is.

Your Money Why is part nature (genetic) and part nurture (environment). You're born with some of it, but the experiences you have as you mature also shape it. So, part of it is intrinsic, and part of it is the image you learn and ultimately project to the world. Your Money Why can evolve or even change with concentrated effort over time.

Your Money Why is essentially driven by what relieves pain and provides pleasure. This is not the same for everyone. And although there are two basic Money Whys (FOMO and FORO), you could have a mix of both. Where you are on the scale has a dramatic impact on how you handle your finances.

Why is this important? Well, because everything or almost everything you do involves money! I just love people who say that money isn't important to them. *Oh really?* Tell me how you spend your day. Tell me what you like to do.

Do you like to take vacations? Money!
Do you wear clothes? Money!
Do you drive a car? Money!
Do you like to eat? Money!

You might argue that you care more about people than money. Okay, tell me about that. How do you "care about people"? Do you love spending time with friends? Yes, me too.

Where do you invite them? To your house? Money!
Do you serve food and drinks? Money!
Are they sitting on chairs? Money!

Unless you're Henry David Thoreau living on the shores of Walden Pond in a one-room cabin, you're gonna need money to live. Granted, some lifestyles require more money than others. None of this is bad. It just is.

We have attached such crazy negative emotions to people who "care about money," and it makes no sense whatsoever. I believe it's a *huge* underlying cause for why people have such a difficult time talking about money. Are there some terrible people out there who care about money above all else? You bet. We call them greedy bastards. They're an unhealthy extreme. But you shouldn't point to them as the reason you can't talk about money in a healthy manner.

A Brief Word About Cake

Another way to look at this is to compare financial personality to having (or lacking) a sweet tooth. I like sweets. I'm not gonna hide the fact that I like a good brownie or piece of chocolate cake. I'm not bad for liking cake. I like cake because it's delicious. When I serve cake to friends, everyone seems pretty darn happy. Now, there are some people in this world who have a cake problem. They want cake all the time. They don't have the cake-moderation gene. Although I often say that's me, it really isn't. Sometimes when I eat too much cake, I get a cake hangover and swear I'll never eat cake again. But we all know that isn't true. Give me a few days and a good chocolate cake, and you'd be wise to hide the forks.

At the other end of the spectrum is the person who can see cake sitting on the kitchen counter and never give it another thought. It's very hard for me to understand these people, but they exist. My mother was one of them. When I was a kid, I thought she was nuts. If I saw a cake on the counter, I thought about it all day. I would count the hours until I could have some for dinner. But my mom was the opposite. She'd make it for us, not for herself. Was I wrong or bad? (I used to think so). Was my mom a good or better person? (I used to think that, too). But she just had a different cake personality than I did. It would have been nice if we'd understood this about each other while she was alive. I hope to help you develop this understanding with your loved ones (not about cake, of course, but money).

Overspenders are a lot like cake lovers. Both do what they do because it gives them pleasure. Buying things and eating cake release dopamine—the hormone and neurotransmitter that triggers the reward center in the brain. It makes us feel good, and it's addictive. On the other hand, savers, like cake haters, don't derive much pleasure from buying things. For whatever reason, they don't get that shot of dopamine from shopping. And some feel superior because of it and let us know that.

The Two Money Whys: FOMO (Fear of Missing Out) and FORO (Fear of Running Out)

FOMOs are hyperfocused on today and discount the future. They are driven by having and doing the things that others have and do. They believe it will make them happy. Whenever someone tells you about their new BMW or their trip to Hawaii, they sound as happy as can be. As we listen to this happy person go on and on about what a great car this is or what a wonderful time they had, of course we want those things too. Who wouldn't? But no one ever mentions the steep monthly payments on that Beemer or the dread that sets in when the bills from that trip arrive and there isn't enough money to pay them. Not so happy then. But we don't see that part.

Social media has created an army of FOMOs. It's driving them to want to "keep up with the Joneses"—to have what they have and to go where they go. But here's the thing, FOMOs: How do you tell if someone *looks* rich or *is* rich? Money is one of the few assets that can be faked. It's easy to tell if someone is tall or thin. With a bit of work, you can usually tell if someone is smart. But rich? Oh, it's so hard. Wouldn't it be great if there were neon signs on people's homes and cars showing how much they owed on them?

FOROs are hyperfocused on the future. They don't care if they're still using a flip phone, clipping coupons, driving a twelve-year-old Prius, or organizing yet another staycation. And for this, they're often misunderstood and mislabeled. They'll be referred to as cheap bastards, stingy, or caring only about money. But that's not true. When they take the Money Is … quiz from chapter 4, they almost always answer, "Money is security." Their underlying emotional driver when it comes to money is financial security for themselves and their family.

While an extreme FOMO needs to have it all, an extreme FORO needs to save it all. FOROs are always worried that no matter how much they've saved, it may disappear in an instant and they'll be living down by the river in a van. They're afraid they will fail their family. Most parents get scared when they don't know where their child is and can't get ahold of them. They worry about the child's safety. FOROs have similar emotions about their financial safety.

FOMO	FORO
Wants to have it all	Wants to save it all
Overspends	Oversaves
Looks rich	Is rich
Wants to impress	Couldn't care less
Not worried	Always worried
Present focused	Future focused
Seeking pleasure	Seeking security

FIND YOUR MONEY WHY

Here's a fun quiz that will help you determine whether you're a FOMO or a FORO. Even if you think you know, take it anyway to be sure and to determine what shade you are:

1. **It's vacation-planning time. You and your partner have been browsing online for weeks, and you've finally made your choice—a ten-day Alaskan cruise (with the unlimited smoked salmon package). You're about to hit the Book It button. At this point, you ...**

    A. Picture the two of you sipping hot toddies on the lido deck as glaciers drift by and whales breach. You look at the calendar and start counting the days. You press the Book It button repeatedly.

    B. Panic a bit. You pause to add up the costs one more time. You check your savings account. You wonder if the expense is really worth it.

2. **A friend passes away unexpectedly. He was your age. After the initial shock, you ...**

    A. Are reminded that life is short. This could have been you. You start a bucket list.

    B. Start worrying if your spouse would be financially okay if you passed away. You check to see if your documents are up to date. You call your financial advisor.

3. **You hear on the news that the stock market has "plummeted." (By the way, on the news, the stock market never goes up or down; it "soars" or "plummets." Perhaps they're trying to get your attention?) You ...**

    A. Turn off the TV or notifications from Fox Business and continue reading *Always Looking Up*, by Michael J. Fox.

B. Immediately log into your account. Start beating yourself up after seeing how much it's down. Consider selling before things get worse.

4. **Your daughter just got accepted at Princeton. Cost is $66,000 per year, after deducting her $10,000 scholarship. She was also accepted by many other great schools with an average annual cost of $42,000. You ...**

A. Immediately buy everyone in the family Princeton polo shirts. You're so proud of her! She's so smart! She's going to be the best anthropologist ever— and the Joneses are going to be so jealous!

B. Start running the numbers. Is it really smart to pay that much money for an anthropology degree? What is she ever going to do with that? You'll have to take out a loan. Or maybe you should ask her to contribute?

5. **Your fifteen-year-old asks for a new phone, even though his current phone is a year old. He insists he must have it. It has a much better camera, and all his friends have one. You ...**

A. Explain to the boy that his phone is fine. When you were his age, phones were mounted to the wall and had ten-foot cords. He complains. He whines. He says everyone will make fun of him. Eventually, you give in.

B. Explain to the boy that his phone is just fine. When you were his age, you just yelled across the street. He complains. He whines. But you stand firm.

6. **You and your partner decide to buy a home. You set a budget, list your must-haves, hire a real estate agent, and start looking. But there's nothing in your price range that has everything you want. So, you ...**

A. Tell the Realtor to expand the search to more expensive homes.

B. Take another look at your must-haves and prioritize them into needs, wants, and wishes. You give the revised list to your Realtor and tell her to stay within the original budget.

7. **You just learned you're having a baby! After looking deeply into each other's eyes, celebrating with some sparkling nonalcoholic cider, and telling everyone the good news, you ...**

A. Order lots of stuff from Amazon for the nursery. "Did you see this double breast pump? It'll be such a time-saver!"

B. Apply for the new job that just opened up at work. (Babies are expensive, and you'll need the extra cash.) Start dropping hints about someone throwing a shower. Call your financial advisor to discuss a college savings plan.

8. **The holidays are coming up. You ...**

   A. Start discussing whether you should invite the whole family over to your house or escape to Punta Cana—just the two of you. The more options you explore, the more excited you get. Don't you just love the holidays?

   B. Start looking forward to some downtime. If Morty from accounting cooperates, you can string together an entire two weeks. How great will that be? Relax. Watch bowl games. Eat queso.

9. **You've been looking for a new job, and you just got called for an interview by the company you're most excited about working for. You ...**

   A. Schedule a haircut and facial and go shopping for a new suit and briefcase. You must look your best!

   B. Do a deep dive into the company. Number of employees? Glassdoor reviews? Does it contribute to employee 401(k)s? Health insurance?

10. **Your brother-in-law, who is always going on fancy vacations and driving new cars, lost his job. For the last six months, he has been sitting around complaining how unfair life is. Now he's asking to "borrow" some money. You ...**

    A. Give it to him. After all, he's your wife's brother, and he's never asked you for anything before. Better to keep the family peace.

    B.   Don't give it to him. Instead, you offer to use your LinkedIn connections to help him find another job. You also refer him to your financial advisor.

11. **Your uncle, who's worked hard his entire life, has been diagnosed with cancer. He will be unable to work for the foreseeable future. His employer will pay some disability, but it won't be enough to live on. You ...**

    A.   Immediately offer your help. You prepare meals for the week and deliver them. You drive him to doctor appointments so his wife can work part time. You mow his lawn. You're a daily resource.

    B.   Immediately offer to help. You put him in touch with a lawyer who may be able to get him more disability payments as well as Social Security disability. You offer him financial assistance until he receives this additional money.

Tally your A and B answers. More A's than B's? You're a FOMO. More B's than A's? You're a FORO. The wider the gap between the A's and B's, the further along the scale for that personality you are.

One of the things you may have noticed about almost all the answers is that they're forward looking. They're gauging your reaction to certain situations. There are no wrong or right answers; it's about how different personalities react to certain situations and think about money. This is the why behind those decisions. For example, remember the first question—the one about the couple planning the Alaskan vacation?

FOMOs (answer A) romanticize the experience. They can already see their social posts and how many likes they'll get. This feedback makes them feel great. Meanwhile, FOROs (answer B) agonize about booking the trip. This is good to a certain extent—they're making sure they can afford it. But if the worry results in their never going anywhere, then that's unfortunate.

Look at the scenario in the second question—a dear friend suddenly passing away. FOMOs (answer A) imagine the same thing happening to them. It's pushing them to live a regret-free life. This feeling—their amygdala kicking in—overrides any thoughts of not having enough money to complete their bucket list. Meanwhile, FOROs (answer B) react more practically, considering the financial situation their loved ones will be left with if this happens to them. Due to the extreme emotion of this type of event, it's a big trigger for both personalities. The amygdala (the feeling brain) drives them both very deep into their Money Whys.

HOW DIFFERENT MONEY WHYS REACT TO …

	FOMO	FORO
Purchasing a car	It has AC in the seats!	I think I spent way too much.
Losing a job	I'll find something else.	I don't know what I'm going to do.
Retiring	Let's go!	We'd better be careful.
Traveling	First class all the way!	Can you fit everything in a carry-on?

Keep in mind, we all have a money personality, or Money Why. It's neither good nor bad. The real question is this: Is your Money Why working for you? Many people may need or just want to change. Before we can figure out how to do that, it's useful to know what specific shade of FOMO or FORO you (and your spouse/partner) are and how your money marriage works. I'll help you answer each of these questions in the next few chapters.

Three Things to Remember from This Chapter

1. There are two basic Money Whys: FOMO (fear of missing out) and FORO (fear of running out).

2. Neither Money Why is good or bad. It just is.

3. Identifying your Money Why is vital to achieving Financial Happiness.

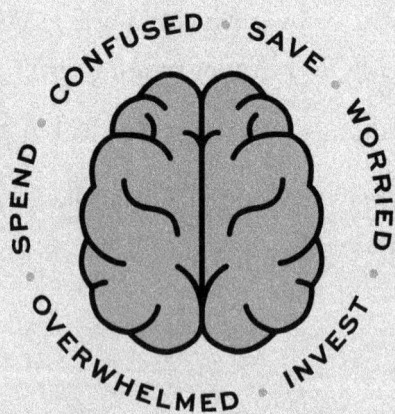

CHAPTER 6

FOUR SHADES OF FOMO

Anyone who lives within their means suffers from a lack of imagination.
—OSCAR WILDE

Hello, FOMOs! Wow, there are a lot of you. But before we begin, did you hear about the cute little tiki bar the Baldwins just built by their pool? It's so fun! As soon as you see it, you're gonna want one. Oh, and before I forget, I just found this great online dress shop called eShakti. You gotta check it out. They'll custom fit anything you buy for just ten dollars extra.

Obviously, I'm playing with you. But if you found yourself wondering where the Baldwins live or typing eShakti.com into your web browser, that only confirms you're a FOMO. However, not all FOMOs are alike; there are shades—four to be exact: the Happy Shopper, the Ostrich, the Regretaholic, and the Look at Me! Identifying your specific shade of FOMO will give you further insight into your financial decisions and help you start making better ones.

In this chapter, I'll explain each shade, give you a real-life example from my practice, and provide a short, fun quiz that can help you determine your shade. (If you're a FORO, you can skip to the next chapter … unless you'd like to learn more about a FOMO in your life.) These four classifications are based on my observations from working with more than five hundred clients over twenty-plus years. The stories that accompany each shade are true, although the clients' names have been changed to protect their privacy.

The Happy Shopper

The Happy Shopper is someone whose brain fires up like one of Elon Musk's SpaceX rockets every time they see a cool new product on their social media feed or get within five miles of Costco. Several motivations can explain the pleasure Happy Shoppers get from their spending sprees. Some people are always buying things for others, and this makes them feel generous, loved, and popular. Bless them. Other people are buying everything so they can look rich. In fact, these folks would often rather look rich than be rich.

Both situations can lead to what some psychiatrists call "compulsive buying disorder." Although not an addiction per se, buying too much, buying things you don't need, and continuing to buy when bad consequences result can have similar negative effects.[36] Don't misunderstand me. I'm not antishopping—it's what makes the economy thrive. But if you spend money you don't have on things you don't need to impress people you don't know, shopping can become a problem.

MEET DEBBIE

Debbie is intelligent and beautiful. She has an executive-level job at a large company. She's well respected and liked by her peers, subordinates, and boss. She has a great work ethic. Debbie does

---

36 Donald W. Black, "A Review of Compulsive Buying Disorder," National Institutes of Health, https://www.ncbi.nlm.nih.gov/pmc/articles/PMC1805733/.

her job well. She is tall and slender, with lovely features and a captivating smile.

From the outside, everybody would agree that Debbie has it all. She seems happily married, has two terrific kids, and lives in a high-end home that is tastefully decorated. She drives a red BMW convertible that everyone envies. She has a bubbly personality and is extremely generous.

But Debbie has a problem she hides from everyone. Well, almost everyone. Her husband and I both know. He seems angry and frustrated. I feel challenged. Despite her high income and successful career, she is spending the money she should be saving for retirement. In fact, she's spending *more* than she's making and running up credit card debt. This isn't anything new. It's always been her pattern. When you're young, it doesn't seem like a problem. But when you're in your midfifties, as Debbie is now, the time is running out to prepare for retirement.

This is a smart woman. Doesn't she realize what's going to happen if she doesn't change her behavior? Of course she does. But I can show her charts, graphs, and a retirement plan until the cows come home, and it won't make any difference. I'm not providing her with information she doesn't already have. So, what am I going to do? I must get to the heart of the problem. I must figure out her sources of pain and pleasure. Although not having enough money for retirement is making her increasingly anxious and sleep deprived, it can't compare to the real source of her pain: *feeling she's not good enough.* That's her Money Why.

Debbie never felt she was pretty enough, successful enough, or rich enough. These insecurities were ingrained in her from a very early age. That's a tough nut to crack because there's no measurable solution. It's never, "I'll be rich enough when I have X." Because there will always be something else, something more. It becomes like the dog chasing its tail. Do you want to look rich or be rich?

WHAT I LOVE ABOUT HAPPY SHOPPERS AND WHAT MAKES ME WORRY

As the name specifies, Happy Shoppers are happy people when they're shopping, and I love that about them. Whether they're buying something for the grandkids or something beautiful for their home, they're excited and bubbly and fun to be around. Happy Shoppers will make you happy, too (unless you're married to one).

But what makes me worry about Happy Shoppers like Debbie is that they're trying to build an image and distract themselves from deeply rooted and often painful feelings. Money can't fix emotional problems. Buying things generates only temporary happiness. Then the doubt, insecurity, and loneliness return. In these cases, the spending gets out of control and jeopardizes long-term goals such as retirement. Some people can't outshop their income, but most can.

THE VOICE IN A HAPPY SHOPPER'S HEAD

- I'm not successful enough.

- Look at that cute purse!

- I'm not smart enough.

- There's a sale on golf clubs!

- I'm not good looking enough.

- Prime Day is next week!

- I'm just not enough.

- That new YETI mug is sweet!

FAVORITE TV SERIES ABOUT HAPPY SHOPPERS

Sex and the City.

(Where do these women even *get* their money?)

QUIZ: ARE YOU A HAPPY SHOPPER?

Tally the number of yes and no answers to the following:

1. Do you know the first name of your Amazon driver?
2. Do you smile when you see a package at the door?
3. Do you feel that if you're not dressed "right," meaning in the latest styles and/or name-brand clothing, people will look down on you?
4. Are you annoyed when you go to someone's house and they have a newer/bigger/nicer kitchen/living room/patio?
5. When you're wearing an expensive suit or dress, do you feel more confident?
6. When you buy a new piece of furniture, does your heart beat faster?
7. After a purchase, are you happier and can't wait to tell someone?
8. Do you live for the words *thank you* when you gift?
9. Does a new purchase lose its excitement/value long before it wears out?
10. Have you ever hidden purchases from a spouse/partner?
11. Have you ever hidden the credit card bill from a spouse/partner?

How many questions did you answer yes to?

4 = mild   6 = moderate   7+ = extreme

The Ostrich

This person enjoys spending money too. But beyond using it for transactional purposes, they don't want anything to do with it. They don't want to think about money, they don't want to talk about money, and they don't want you to ask them about money. They find financial conversations extremely stressful. They're frequently worried they're making bad financial decisions, so they try not to make any. However, we're all making these decisions every day. Every time we buy something or don't buy something, it's a financial decision. The Ostrich is usually afraid that if they're forced into a financial discussion, the person they're talking to will take away their ability to spend money.

The Ostrich lives for today. When I have one in my office and I tell them that they're spending too much, they get anxious (as opposed to a Happy Shopper, who'll get angry). Their Money Why usually stems from a family where horrible financial things happened. Maybe a parent hid debt, gambled, or just made terrible financial choices. So, whenever a big financial decision looms, the Ostrich sticks their head in the ground to avoid resurrecting that pain and fear.

MEET TOM AND NANCY

Tom and Nancy own and operate a successful business. Nancy inherited it from her parents and has worked there since she was young. Her parents were responsible with money and included her and her siblings in financial discussions. They had financial advisors, accountants, and lawyers, and they shared all this information with Nancy.

Tom's family was a different story. He had a stay-at-home mom and a father with a good job in sales. But his dad liked to gamble. This did not work out well. His losses compounded over the years until he had to sell the family house and downsize to a smaller home. They had only enough money to just get by. Tom had a front-row seat to his mom's tears and his parents' arguments. He still carries these scars today and gets anxious when he has to talk about money.

As her financial advisor, I see Nancy regularly. Tom rarely attends our meetings. Nancy says he never looks at any of their financial statements or asks questions. He is a smart, hardworking, and educated guy. You can talk to Tom about a variety of topics because he is well read and interesting. But when it comes to money, particularly *his* money, he shuts down.

WHAT I LOVE ABOUT OSTRICHES AND WHAT MAKES ME WORRY

Ostriches are clever enough to find ways of protecting themselves from the pain of dealing with money. Because they don't want to argue about it like their parents did, they avoid it. They put their trust in someone else to handle it. Trust is a huge component to relationships and happiness. But with Ostriches, the trust goes too far. They often put their trust in someone they shouldn't, or the person they trust dies and they're lost. When it comes to money, you should never do something for someone else that they should be doing for themselves.

THE VOICE IN AN OSTRICH'S HEAD

- I can't stand talking about money.

- Discussions about money always end in a fight.

- I'm not capable of handling money.

- I'm not smart enough to oversee the finances.

- If I don't do anything, someone else will.

FAVORITE MOVIE CLIP ABOUT AN OSTRICH

Jumanji: The Next Level

(Has nothing to do with money, but it's the best ostrich chase scene you'll ever see: https://www.youtube.com/watch?v=duM4ILMieiU.)

QUIZ: ARE YOU AN OSTRICH?

Tally the number of yes and no answers to the following:

1. Would you rather go to the dentist than a financial advisor?
2. Does reviewing your finances give you anxiety?
3. Do you insist that your spouse/partner handle all financial matters?
4. Do you insist that your spouse/partner pay the bills?
5. You're at the pro shop and you see a putter you really like. Do you ignore the price and purchase it?
6. Do you ignore your spouse's/partner's requests to review the budget with you?

7. Do you frequently worry about the finances but distract yourself with something until the feelings go away?

8. Do you assume everyone else is better off than you?

How many questions did you answer yes to?

2 = mild   4 = moderate   6+ = extreme

The Regretaholic

The Regretaholic lives by the words *Life is short, and I don't want to miss out on anything.* Their bucket list is bottomless. Their favorite book is *Die Broke.* They're extremely envious of anybody who is going somewhere they haven't been, buying a car they don't have, owning a house that's bigger than theirs, etc. They believe that if they were to experience or own these things, they would feel extreme happiness. So, they are always in the regret phase, always chasing something. They don't want to focus on retirement financial needs, and they hate facing the fact that at some point they may need money for long-term care. What they don't realize is that true happiness is the quality of your life minus envy.

The Money Why driving Regretaholics is usually a parent or friend who died early and didn't get to enjoy life fully. Or sometimes they may have had an extremely poor childhood, and now that they're semisuccessful, they want (and feel entitled to) everything. It's an emotional thought pattern that runs deep.

MEET BARB AND PAUL JEAN

They met in France. It was Barb's first visit, but Paul Jean worked there. They immediately hit it off. They shared many interests and the same sense of humor. They felt like they had known each other forever.

When her vacation ended, Barb returned to the States. She had a good job at a company she'd been with for years. Her grown children lived nearby. She spoke with and emailed Paul Jean frequently. Their romance continued. Although his family was originally from France, he and his family had moved to the States some time ago. Paul Jean decided to visit them and explore job opportunities. As luck and love would have it, they ended up getting engaged and eventually married.

As the years passed, Barb and Paul Jean always reminisced about their storybook time in France. They vowed to return one day and live there for a while. But neither one had saved much. Their previous marriages had ended in divorce, and that had been expensive. But they really wanted to do this before some health or life problem interfered, so they tapped their retirement accounts and rented a lovely cottage in Provence for two years.

It was the best time of their lives. The food! The wine! Those chocolate-filled croissants! But the money lasted only so long before they realized they'd have to return to the States to find jobs and start rebuilding their nest eggs. This is when I met them. They were starting from almost zero in their fifties. I remember saying to Barb, "You must worry about money all the time." To which she replied, "No, not really. I'll be fine. It'll work out."

I couldn't decide whether to love or hate her. I know I was jealous of that mindset. I sooooo don't have that. This was almost twenty years ago, and to this day they don't regret their decision. They are neither crazy nor stupid. They continue to work into their seventies because full retirement isn't an option. They've built up some funds, but it's not enough. They could have saved more, but they continue to spend. And they don't regret their decisions. They're on the same page with their financial choices. I worry way more about their future than they do. What if someone has a health crisis? What if something happens and they need funds? I could go on. I decided to love them.

WHAT I LOVE ABOUT REGRETAHOLICS AND WHAT MAKES ME WORRY

Because they've gone places and done things, Regretaholics are great at cocktail parties. They have a zest for life, and they live in the present—goals that many of us have but few obtain. They have T-shirts that say carpe diem ("seize the day") or maybe just mugs. My worry comes when this happy-go-lucky personality goes too far. You must live for today, but you must also plan for tomorrow. Regretaholics are all about *the now.* No matter how much they don't want to think about it, there will come a time when they need retirement money or long-term care. By then, their earning years will be over and their options limited. The last thing anyone needs at the end of life is financial worries or, ironically, the regret that they didn't save enough money.

THE VOICE IN A REGRETAHOLIC'S HEAD

- Who knows? I could die tomorrow.

- Everyone else is having fun—I want to have fun too.

- I'll be so happy if I take this around-the-world cruise.

- It's only money.

- I'll be fine; things always work out.

FAVORITE MOVIE ABOUT REGRETAHOLICS

The Bucket List

(Jack Nicholson and Morgan Freeman will make you laugh—and cry.)

QUIZ: ARE YOU A REGRETAHOLIC?

Tally the number of yes and no answers to the following:

1. Friends tell you about their upcoming hiking trip in Switzerland. Is this all you can think about for the next few days?
2. You're out shopping and see a beautiful, handmade, live-edge dining room table. Do you buy it immediately?
3. When you hear about a friend having a heart attack, do you think you might be next?
4. You have a heart attack. Do you have regrets over the places you haven't been and the things you didn't do?
5. When you decide to make a major purchase (e.g., car, vacation, home renovation), do you buy first and talk to your financial advisor later?
6. Is your goal to die with zero dollars in the bank?
7. When a friend comes to you worried that they shouldn't have bought something, do you reassure them everything will be fine?
8. Do you focus more on friends and family who have died early as opposed to those who are living a long life?
9. Do you generally feel good about your decisions to spend money?

How many questions did you answer yes to?

3 = mild   5 = moderate   7+ = extreme

The Look at Me!

The Look at Me! would rather look rich than be rich. Their self-worth is largely based on their material possessions. This is the guy on the Strip with the Rolex and Rivian. This is the woman in Saint-Tropez with the Manolos sipping Veuve Clicquot. The "it girl" and the "it guy." No doubt you've heard the phrase *keeping up with the Joneses*. Well, these are the Joneses. Owning the best makes them feel like the best, and they want you to notice them. Like Happy Shoppers, their Money Why is a deep insecurity that materialism helps them mask or forget.

The problem with this mindset is that the goalposts in this game of material one-upmanship are constantly moving. There's always new tech. There are always fancier cars. There are always trendier vacation spots and more fashionable clothes.

Becoming the Joneses—or just keeping up with them—has been a major emotional driver of spending since caveman days. ("Torg has big club; me need bigger one.") But when you stop to think about it, we really didn't know a whole lot about the Joneses until recently. You knew the house (or cave) they lived in, the cars (or woolly mammoths) they drove, and that was about it. But then came social media, and now we know what everybody owns because it's broadcast every single day. The "I-want-what-she's-having" mindset isn't just a line from the movie *When Harry Met Sally*.

MEET SAM AND KATHY

Sam and Kathy are both college graduates with advanced degrees and good jobs. They married in their twenties and make a handsome couple. Their country-club wedding was spectacular. A string quartet played during the ceremony, and a live band rocked the reception. There were ice sculptures, an artist doing an oil painting, and a live flower wall.

Sam and Kathy work at a hospital with surgeons who have much higher incomes than they do. They desperately wanted the surgeons' lifestyle. So, they bought a beautiful home and mortgaged themselves to the hilt. A few years later, they started a family. Kathy quickly returned to work after each pregnancy because her income was essential. They were smart and hardworking. But as their income grew, so did their expenses. They bought fancy cars. They put in a magnificent pool with an outdoor kitchen. They took family vacations to expensive resorts. They loved posting on social media about their ski trip to Vail and their bike tour in Tuscany. They liked fine wines and Michelin-star restaurants.

What hasn't been mentioned so far? Oh, they didn't save for their kids' college education or, oops, their own retirement. They figured they would take care of those things later. With college, they got lucky. Each of the kids got substantial athletics scholarships. But now they're in their fifties, and their luck is running out. They asked me to put a retirement plan together. Given the income level they enjoyed for thirty years, their savings amount was small.

As a rule of thumb, you can withdraw $40,000 per year from a retirement portfolio for every $1 million you've saved. Sam and Kathy had been living on $20,000 *per month* net, or $240,000 a year. That means they needed $6 million in the bank before they could retire. These numbers may seem crazy to some people, but this couple had been earning a combined $400,000 per year. When I told them they didn't have enough to retire on, they were shocked, dismayed, and a bit angry. They directed some of that anger at each other. Previously, they didn't seem to blame one another for anything. They enjoyed sharing stories of all the wonderful things they'd done and bought. But this was different. Suddenly, their marriage was in crisis.

Sam and Kathy must now face the reality of saving extreme amounts of money every year, working into their seventies, and/or dramatically changing their lifestyle. I've been down this road with other people before, and I can tell you that getting anyone to change their lifestyle in retirement is very difficult. We all get used to our lifestyles—whether it's taking vacations or going out to dinner or wearing nice clothes or living in a lovely home. Trading down is hard. It embarrasses us. These are difficult emotions to handle.

WHAT I LOVE ABOUT THE LOOK AT ME! AND WHAT MAKES ME WORRY

The Look at Me! is willing to work hard to get what they want (or willing to work hard to marry someone who works hard so they can get what they want). They crave attention and change and are naturally curious. The worry is that, because the goalposts keep moving, they cannot be happy or content. (Indeed, if having a glamorous life created happiness, why are so many famous people dreadfully unhappy, divorced, or even drug addicts?) Because the Look at Me! hasn't figured out what drives Financial Happiness, they're busy spending money they don't have on things they don't need to impress people they don't know. They never feel satisfaction. And this has even deeper personal ramifications.

When they see someone who has things they don't own or are going places they haven't been, it makes them feel "less than." They may admire these people, but at the same time they feel very bad for themselves and that they're not doing enough. It can be a vicious, soul-destroying cycle.

THE VOICE IN THE LOOK AT ME!'S HEAD

- I'm not enough.

- I *need* a bigger house in a better neighborhood.

- I'm not working hard enough; I need to do more.

- I'm not as good as the next guy because he's been to the Super Bowl and I haven't.

- Everyone will know I'm a loser if I don't drive a Porsche.

- I have an image to uphold!

FAVORITE MOVIE ABOUT THE LOOK AT ME!

Crazy Rich Asians

QUIZ: ARE YOU A LOOK AT ME!?

Tally the number of yes and no answers to the following:

1. When you meet someone with a nicer house, do you start figuring out how to buy one like it?
2. When you get a new car or go on vacation, are you anxious to tell everyone about it?
3. When you move into a beautiful home, are you telling yourself you're winning?
4. When you see something that someone else has, do you tell yourself you *deserve* that?

5. When someone shares a great trip they took, are you telling yourself, *My trip was better*?
6. When you go to an event, do you want to be the best dressed one there?
7. When you're at that event, do you make sure everyone knows you're wearing Gucci?
8. Are you always looking for a bigger house, a better car, nicer jewelry?
9. Is the title you hold at work very important to you?
10. Would it thrill you to be given your own parking space?

How many questions did you answer yes to?

3 = mild   5 = moderate   7+ = extreme

Conclusion

So, by now you should know what type of FOMO you are. If it's unclear (e.g., maybe you relate to both the Regretaholic and Look at Me!), don't worry. Human beings don't always fit neatly into a box. There are shades to every Money Why, and these shades can change over time. Look for the type of FOMO where you got the most extreme rating. So, if you're an extreme Happy Shopper and a moderate Ostrich, your main Money Why is the former.

Knowing this is a huge step. Up until now, your Money Why has been subconsciously influencing every money decision you made. It's why you're in the financial situation you're in, for better or worse. Going forward, I want you to be *conscious* of these underlying emotions whenever you're making an important money decision. For example ...

- If you're a Happy Shopper, ask yourself *why* you're really buying whatever it is you're buying.

- If you're an Ostrich, ask yourself *why* you're not joining your spouse for the annual review with your financial advisor.

- If you're a Regretaholic, ask yourself *why* you're so scared of missing out.

- If you're a Look at Me!, ask yourself *why* getting ten thousand Instagram followers is so important to you.

Three Things to Remember from This Chapter

1. There are four FOMO subsets: Happy Shopper, Ostrich, Regretaholic, and Look at Me! Which one are you?

2. As a rule of thumb, you can withdraw $40,000 per year from a retirement portfolio for every $1 million you've saved.

3. True happiness equals the quality of your life minus envy.

CHAPTER 7

THREE SHADES OF FORO

Money is not the most important thing in the
world. Love is. Fortunately, I love money.
—JACKIE MASON

Hello, FOROs! I know exactly how you feel about money because I was a FORO myself. My parents were raised during the Great Depression, and I inherited many of their penny-pinching ways. I still use one tea bag all day long. Up until four or five years ago, I refused to waste money on Christmas tree ornaments. I made my own. And don't get me started on pantyhose … when my expensive pantyhose got the runs, I didn't throw them away. No, I'd cut off the leg with the run and keep doing that until I had one pair with a good right leg and another with a good left leg. Then I'd put them on together! Let me tell you, I could have been the editor of the *Cheapskate Gazette*.

Not all FOROs are alike, however. There are different shades—three to be exact: the Miser, the Security Seeker, and the Eeyore. Identifying your specific shade of FORO will give you further insight into your financial decisions and help you start making better ones.

In this chapter, I'll explain each shade, provide a real-life example drawn from my practice, and give a short, fun quiz so you can decide if that's you. (If you're a FOMO, you can skip to the next chapter … unless you'd like to learn more about a FORO in your life.) These three classifications are based on my observations from working with more than five hundred clients over twenty-plus years. The stories that accompany each one are true, although the names have been changed to protect their privacy.

The Miser

The Miser has two prominent traits that coexist. One is an extreme fear of running out of money, and the other is a tremendous sense of pride as their account balance grows. It can be very difficult for Misers to spend money on anything. They typically drive their cars until they rust out. When they do buy a new car, they worry that they paid too much or were foolish with their money. They have buyer's remorse.

Some Misers can be extremely private about their money, like the guy who gives himself haircuts but shocks everyone when he bequeaths millions to his alma mater. Other Misers enjoy sharing advice on saving, investing, and building something from nothing. In either case, their Money Why usually stems from an impoverished childhood or some financially disastrous experience. They are generally pessimists.

MEET BOB

Bob's parents lived through the Great Depression and World War II. He was taught the value of a dollar and of hard work. He was the first one in his family to go to college, earning a degree in engineering from Penn State. He graduated in 1976 when the economy was struggling and jobs were scarce, but he was hired by a Fortune 500 firm. His starting salary was $10,300 per year, already more than his father made after decades at the manufacturing plant. Everyone was proud.

Bob leased an apartment close to work. Between his student debt, the rent, and other living expenses, things were tight. He maintained the austere lifestyle he had experienced growing up. He saved money and slowly paid off his loans. Eventually, he met a wonderful woman named Carol, and they married within a year. They wanted a family and a home, so they had a very modest wedding—a few guests and a reception at his in-laws' place. After a year, they'd saved enough for a down payment on a house—very similar to the small Cape Cod–style home he grew up in. Bob was proud of what he had accomplished by age twenty-six. Within another year, they had the first of two children. Given the cost of daycare, Carol quit her job and stayed home. It was a smart financial decision.

As time passed, Bob received many promotions, and his earnings soared. He took great delight in tracking his conservative investments month by month and seeing his portfolio grow. Carol thought that with a growing family and money in the bank, they could get a larger house. Bob refused.

Fast-forward thirty-five years. They still live in the same house. They have no debt. Their car is thirteen years old. Bob doesn't like wasting money on eating out or going on vacations. He questions every dollar that's spent. He maintains strict control of all the finances. In the process, he and Carol have become multimillionaires. They have more than enough for a comfortable, worry-free retirement. But Bob is still anxious they'll run out and refuses to buy anything or go anywhere. Carol is increasingly unhappy, feeling that life is passing them by.

WHAT I LOVE ABOUT MISERS AND WHAT MAKES ME WORRY

I admire Bob's dedication to investing and finances. He did everything correctly. But I worry that Carol is right: life *is* passing them by. They're missing the joyous experience of family vacations. They're missing the pleasure of upgrading their living space with more comfortable furniture and maybe a big TV. But most of all, I worry that Bob will never be content. You can't hit a target you don't have. It's just the unending desire for a bigger and bigger bottom line. He's confusing his self-worth with his net worth.

THE VOICE IN A MISER'S HEAD

- They don't make things like they used to.

- Everyone thinks they're better than me because they have more money. I'll show them.

- If I can just double this money, I'll be happy.

- I must work harder.

- I must save more.

FAVORITE MOVIE ABOUT MISERS

A Christmas Carol

(Of course)

QUIZ: ARE YOU A MISER?

Tally the number of yes and no answers to the following:

1. Have you ever bought clothing from the Salvation Army (or similar secondhand store)?
2. Have you ever pumped windshield wiper fluid back into the bottle before trading in a car?
3. Do you keep your car longer than ten years, even though you can afford to replace it?
4. Do you get miffed when the bank lowers your interest rate on savings, even though you know all interest rates are going down?
5. Do you have to control every purchase made in the house, regardless of what it's for?
6. Do you *hate* to mow the lawn but refuse to pay someone to do it, even though you can afford it?
7. Do you get upset if you arrive too late for the early-bird special?
8. When your spouse/partner or kids ask you to buy something for them, is your immediate response, "You don't need that."
9. Are you wearing a T-shirt from twenty-five years ago? If not, is it only because it doesn't fit?

How many questions did you answer yes to?

3 = mild   5 = moderate   7+ = extreme

The Security Seeker

The Security Seeker feels a deep sense of responsibility. They want to make sure their family will never have to worry about money. They are the provider *and* the protector. Unlike Misers, Security Seekers are not saving money to see it grow—their focus is making sure their loved ones are well cared for. It is a noble endeavor, but it is primarily driven by fear and, perhaps, memories of a father leaving the family or a single mother dying young. Deep insecurity is their Money Why.

The Security Seeker is afraid that something will happen and their savings will disappear. They may be worried about losing their job, the next election, or some cataclysmic event. Whatever it is, they think their investments could evaporate in an instant. They have great difficulty learning to handle market volatility. They love having lots of money in their checking and savings accounts, even if it's earning little or no interest. They usually have cash stashed somewhere in the house.

MEET MARTI

Marti grew up in a modest home in Ithaca, New York. It was the typical 1960s household. Her dad was a salesman for a large construction company; her mom was a housekeeper. Her dad's income was enough to support the family comfortably. Her mom was in charge of all the finances and oversaw the family budget like a drill sergeant. She taught Marti and her siblings the difference between needs and wants. She felt their needs were few. If it wasn't on sale, you didn't need it.

In grade school, Marti opened a passbook savings account. (For those of you under a hundred, this was a program coordinated by schools and local banks where you recorded your deposits and balance in a little booklet.) When Marti got money for her birthday or on a holiday, she'd put it in her savings account. Whenever she showed the book to her mother, she'd be showered with praise: "I'm so proud that you're saving for a rainy day!"

This was an outstanding lesson in delayed gratification. It was also a lesson in fear. You never know what might happen. Smart people are careful with money and save as much as possible. Marti got a memorable example of this when her dad got laid off. The "rainy day" had arrived, but fortunately her parents had been saving.

Marti was fifteen at the time and took a job busing tables at the local diner to help out. She felt mature, responsible, and grown-up. Her parents reinforced those feelings.

As an adult, Marti continued adding to her savings and her retirement accounts every year, no matter what. She taught her kids the difference between needs and wants. They lived in their original house—they didn't *need* a new one. They repaired their appliances—they didn't *need* new ones. Under pressure from her husband and kids, they occasionally went on vacation, but they would save up for it. Credit card balances were a hard no.

In today's influencer-driven world, Marti's family became less and less content with denying their wants. They couldn't see that it was Marti's immense love for them and her desire to keep them "safe" that was driving her stingy behavior. "You never know when a rainy day will come," she'd tell them.

WHAT I LOVE ABOUT SECURITY SEEKERS AND WHAT MAKES ME WORRY

I love that Marti cares so deeply for her family and doesn't waste money. Every family needs an air bag. But I worry that she has taken it too far. She is overly focused on what *could* happen to her family rather than what *is* happening to her family. Life is a balance. Having security is great, but a little risk is fine. While planning for the future, you can't forget about the present. Spending and saving *are not* an either/or proposition. You can do both and still be financially happy.

THE VOICE IN A SECURITY SEEKER'S HEAD

- Do I have enough money if something happens?

- I should check my account balance.

- I'm the responsible one in this family. Otherwise, we'd be broke!

- I'm not gonna let my family go through what my parents did.

- I think someone is taking money from the coffee can.

FAVORITE MOVIE ABOUT SECURITY SEEKERS

Don't Look Up

(For Security Seekers, there's always a comet looming on the horizon.)

QUIZ: ARE YOU A SECURITY SEEKER?

Tally the number of yes and no answers to the following:

1. Do you check your account balances weekly?
2. Do you get anxious when someone in your family wants to make a big purchase?
3. Do you get anxious when you must make a big purchase?
4. Are you always concerned you're not saving enough?
5. Do you frequently imagine scenarios of bad things happening?

6. Do you feel it's your responsibility to make sure your kids get good-paying jobs?

7. Do you feel you're the best person to teach your kids about financial responsibility?

8. Are you shocked when you discover that other people aren't saving for retirement?

9. When you see friends or neighbors buying a new car every few years, are you extremely curious as to how they afford it?

10. When you discover that someone wasn't prepared for a financial event, do you think, *I told you so.*

How many questions did you answer yes to?

3 = mild   5 = moderate   7+ = extreme

The Eyore

We all know the Eyore. Like Winnie-the-Pooh's sad donkey pal, this person is a champion worrier. If their car breaks down, they immediately worry it'll cost a lot to fix or it won't be fixable at all and they'll have to buy a new one. Eeyores tend to be pessimists and have a sort of learned helplessness. They can find a cloud on a sunny day. Their defining characteristics are 1) they believe bad events are inevitable, 2) they're sure these bad events will destroy any goals they have, and 3) they're convinced everything is their fault. Their Money Why usually stems from a family member or even a teacher who constantly berated them and made them feel worthless and inadequate. With such a woe-is-me attitude, Eeyores tend to give up easily and feel depressed. "Don't worry about me," Eeyore tells Pooh. "Go and enjoy yourself. I'll stay here and be miserable."

MEET DAVE

Dave's always been a loner. He never participated in school activities. He felt no one wanted to hang out with him, but he was fine with that. He preferred to stay home, read, and watch sports. He believed that no one is truly happy.

But Dave is intelligent and a hard worker. He graduated college with a degree in computer science. He was recruited by lots of companies and landed a job at a large firm. But it wasn't long before he became unhappy. His supervisors often disagreed with him. Even though this is something that happens to everyone, he felt singled out and stupid. He wished he hadn't taken the job, but there was no sense looking for a new one because they probably wouldn't like him either.

Dave worked up the courage to ask a young woman out. To his surprise, she said yes, and they hit it off. Eventually, they married. (It took him a long time to propose because he was certain she'd say no.) They purchased a home, and after years passed, they came to see me about developing a retirement plan. Their dream was to retire early.

In working through their finances, I noticed they were quite frugal. Their mortgage was almost paid off. They didn't have any car loans or credit card debt. They had a lot of money sitting in bank accounts earning little interest but only one investment account (Dave's 401(k)). The cash in the bank far exceeded what they needed for emergencies. I told them it's almost impossible to save your way to retirement with no return on your money. I asked why they hadn't been investing. Dave explained that he tried playing the stock market once but had lost money. "I'm a terrible investor," he said, "and the whole system is rigged against us little guys."

His wife said very little during these meetings. Over the years, she'd tried to get him to be more optimistic but had failed. He handled the money. I made it clear that if they continued on this path, early retirement was out of the question. It took me quite a while to convince him to get more growth oriented with his investments. His wife's support and constant reassurance have been a big help. I also believe that having me make the investment decisions gives him some relief—although he is always the first to call when the market drops.

WHAT I LOVE ABOUT EEYORES AND WHAT MAKES ME WORRY

I love Eeyores for trying to do the right thing for themselves and their families. They stay at a job they hate because they feel it's the responsible thing to do. They live within their means and save money for the future. But they just can't get out of their own way. Their pessimistic nature drives them to give up easily. If they make a bad decision, they feel it's further proof that they're a bad decision-maker. When something in life goes awry, they feel it's one more sign that they're a poor planner. If it wasn't for his wife and me, I worry Dave would sink into depression. Most financial decisions are based on the future. If you don't see a nice future, it can be hard to prepare for it.

THE VOICE IN AN EEYORE'S HEAD

- Everything I do is wrong.

- I never make the right decisions.

- It doesn't matter what I do; it's never going to get any better.

- No one cares about me.

- The whole system is rigged, so why should I invest?

FAVORITE MOVIE ABOUT EEYORES

The Many Adventures of Winnie the Pooh

QUIZ: ARE YOU AN EEYORE?

Tally the number of yes and no answers to the following:

1. If you receive a gift from a secret admirer, do you assume it was delivered to you by mistake?
2. If you buy a stock and its price falls, do you think you're a bad investor?
3. If your boss yells at you, do you go home and ruminate about how you're probably going to lose your job?
4. If you forget an event you were supposed to attend, do you tell yourself you're terrible at remembering things?
5. If you prepare a meal for friends and they pick at it, do you assume you're a bad cook?
6. Do you always carry an umbrella in your car?
7. When your family plans a vacation, do you spend a lot of time making lists of things that could go wrong?
8. When you hire a workman and they don't show, do you tell yourself you're terrible at hiring these people?
9. When you go on a job interview and don't get the job, do you blame yourself?
10. If you took out a loan to buy a car and the interest rate dropped the following month, do you think you're terrible at financial decisions?

How many questions did you answer yes to?

3 = mild   5 = moderate   7+ = extreme

Conclusion

So, by now you should know what type of FORO you are. If it's unclear (maybe you're a mix of Miser and Security Seeker), don't worry. Human beings don't always fit neatly into a box. There are shades of everything, and they can change. The key thing to look for is the type of FORO where you got the most extreme rating. So, if you're an extreme Eeyore and a moderate Miser, your main Money Why is the former.

Knowing this is a huge step. Up until now your Money Why has been subconsciously influencing every money decision you made. This is why you're in the financial situation you're in, for better or worse. Going forward, I want you to be *conscious* of these underlying emotions whenever you're making an important money decision. For example …

- If you're a Miser, ask yourself *why* you enjoy checking your account balance so often.

- If you're a Security Seeker, ask yourself *why* you're so pessimistic about the future.

- If you're an Eeyore, ask yourself *why* you're always so down on yourself when it comes to money.

Three Things to Remember from This Chapter

1. There are three FORO subsets: Miser, Security Seeker, and Eeyore. Which one are you?

2. Don't confuse your self-worth with your net worth.

3. While planning for the future, don't forget about the present.

CHAPTER 8

YOUR MONEY MARRIAGE

Love is blind, but marriage is a real eye-opener.

—PAULINE THOMASON

C hances are, you're not in this alone. You're married or have a partner who you make financial decisions with. This complicates things. Indeed, spending money foolishly is the second-biggest reason for divorce (infidelity is first),[37] and I'm guessing it's probably the source of most arguments—right up there with how to load the dishwasher.

It's amazing how many couples come into my office for the first time, and when I start talking about financial goals and plans, I can tell they've never discussed this with each other before. These aren't newlyweds; these are couples who have been together for over thirty years. There are two possible reasons for this: 1) talking about money is uncomfortable, or 2) they assume they both want the same thing financially and there's no need to discuss it.

---

37 Mark Travers, "The 6 Top Causes of Divorce," *Psychology Today*, July 15, 2024, https://www.psychologytoday.com/us/blog/social-instincts/202407/ the-6-leading-causes-of-divorce.

SURVEY *SAYS*

HOW OFTEN DO YOU HAVE A FINANCIAL DISCUSSION WITH YOUR SPOUSE/ PARTNER?*

Regularly = **61%**

Rarely/only when necessary = **39%**

*From a 2024 survey of 212 clients conducted by Evans Wealth Strategies

To have adult discussions about money and come to reasonable compromises, you must remove the shame, blame, and guilt that often surrounds money. Now that you know your Money Why, it's time to identify your partner's. This will help you gauge your financial compatibility, allow you to break through emotional barriers in your relationship, and start making progress.

Begin by asking your better half to take the quiz in chapter 5 to determine if they're a FOMO or a FORO. Then have them use either chapter 6 or 7 to identify their shade.

Generally, there are three broad combinations:

- FORO—FORO (saver/saver)

- FOMO—FOMO (spender/spender)

- FOMO—FORO (spender/saver)

When you understand the why behind your approach to money *and* the why behind your loved one's approach to money, you'll finally be on the road to greater Financial Happiness. Plus—bonus!—you'll probably improve your relationship. The goal is for each partner to develop a compassionate attitude toward the other's money behaviors.

Let's take a closer look at each type of relationship …

FORO—FORO

This is a financial advisor's dream. I'm not saying it's the best combination or the one where both partners feel the most fulfilled; it's just that from my perspective it's the easiest to identify and deal with, although it's not that common. I can usually tell within fifteen minutes whether I have this combo. I just need the answers to three questions.

These questions are *not* the following:

- How much money have the two of you saved?

- How much money do you earn?

- Where is your money invested?

The answers to those questions give me numbers, and although they would tell me a lot, I'm initially more interested in a couple's money behaviors than how much they have. So, here's what I ask:

- How long do you typically keep your cars?

- Do you pay off your credit card balances each month?

- How long have you had your house?

In case you haven't figured this out by now, let me give you the answers to these questions. Most FORO—FOROs keep their cars an average of eight to ten years. They never carry credit card debt, "except for that time when our basement flooded, and we were waiting on the check from the insurance company." (It's funny, because they'll immediately share all the details of the incident as a way of absolving themselves of guilt. That's when I know their desire to be super safe with money runs deep.) As for their homes, they stay in them a long time. This is not the couple who trades up with their income level.

When I get these answers, I know my work will mostly be math. If they're not on track for retirement or other goals, I just need to devise a plan they can follow to get there. And they follow direction very well. However, it is not all sunshine and roses. FOROs often have difficulty believing they have enough money to retire on. I typically have to meet with them several times and show them the plan repeatedly before they feel comfortable. They've become so used to saving and building their nest egg that the shift to withdrawing and spending can be tough.

To a saver, making a deposit to a 401(k) every month is like getting a pat on the back. You're doing a great job! You're making fantastic progress! Keep it up! Losing that can be stressful. They may have been saving for forty or fifty years, watching their money grow, and now I'm telling them to stop doing that and start taking money out? It can be a hard habit to break.

I never underestimate the emotional difficulty surrounding this. Although I can confidently tell them they're going to be fine, I empathize with their struggle. As a recovering FORO, I could have retired years ago, but I'm still working (probably harder than ever). I tell people that's because I love my job, and that is absolutely true. But I also know, inside this crazy brain of mine, that the thought of withdrawing money from my accounts is slightly terrifying. I'm proud of having been a good saver and investor. When I withdraw money from my account for anything, I get slightly nauseous, as if I'm doing something wrong. This stems from growing up poor and having numerous encounters with the rug puller. I joke that I have "bag lady syndrome." Although it makes no sense, I'm always slightly scared that everything I've built will go away and I'll be pushing a shopping cart full of aluminum cans down Broad Street. So, I never judge anyone for the emotions they have around money. Everyone has them.

Overall, I find that FORO—FORO couples get along pretty well, at least regarding finances. They seem to agree on most everything and rarely have money arguments. Indeed, if saving for retirement were a sport, they'd both be wearing the same team jersey. They're always pumped up for their annual meeting with me, and if it's been a good market year and they're closer to their goals, I half expect them to high-five right there in the office. But instead of doing something to celebrate, like finally renovating that old bathroom or taking the grandkids to Disney (which I encourage), they say, "No, we're fine" and hustle out to get seated before the early-bird special expires.

The downside to this type of relationship is that sometimes they haven't spent any money on things that provide pleasure today, which is part of Financial Happiness. Extreme FOROs may have never traveled out of state, updated their home, or otherwise rewarded themselves. As we age and see our friends and family members develop health problems or pass away, being so careful with money can lead to regrets. One of the fun things I do is encourage these couples to travel. It takes some convincing and (of course!) a budget, but I've found that after they do it once, they're hooked. Then I have the pleasure of putting aside money in their plan for a trip every year.

FOMO—FOMO

This combo is my biggest challenge as a financial advisor. These couples are enjoying life. I mean *really* enjoying life. Their travel agent is one of their best friends, and if they see something they like, they buy it. They gauge whether they can afford something by how much credit is left on their Visa card. When they come to see me, it's more of a social visit. They don't want to talk about their retirement plan; they want to tell me about their trip to Iceland. To verify their Money Whys, I go back to my three magic questions:

- How long do you typically keep your cars?
- Do you pay off your credit card balances each month?
- How long have you had your house?

Most FOMO—FOMOs either lease their vehicles or buy new ones every few years. They give no thought to the cost ramifications between those options. When I ask what brand of car they drive, it's usually high end. As for credit cards, they always have an ongoing balance, but they try to justify this by listing unusual expenses like a child's wedding or by pointing out they pay more than the minimum each month, so it's okay. They do not realize the long-term financial impact of paying 18 percent interest. And their home? It's usually the biggest and nicest one on the block. They can afford the monthly mortgage, but they're not trying to pay it off early. When repairs or renovations are needed, they tap their home equity line of credit.

Let me be clear, these are *not* bad people. They're generous, and they're a hoot to hang out with. They are not deadbeats with bad credit. They pay their bills; they have successful careers. In fact, part of the reason they spend so much is that they're hard workers and feel they deserve rewards.

So, why are they coming to see me?

There's been a triggering event:

- A layoff
- A healthcare crisis
- A pending retirement

FOMO—FOMOs are usually in their fifties or sixties when they sit down on my sofa. This is usually the first time they've had a serious discussion about their financial goals and identified their retirement needs and wants. Up until now, they didn't know (or care) whether they were on track. And in most cases, they're not. Very few average-income working couples can afford *everything*. That's why I call this initial get-together the "meet Jesus meeting." They're going to have to become at least partial FOROs for the foreseeable future if they're going to make it. No more car leases, no more credit card debt, no more going out to restaurants three or four times a week ... It'll be tough. They'll need to shift their focus from the present to the future. This can be challenging as they learn this new skill. And it often tests the relationship.

FOMO—FORO

It's true that opposites attract. This is the most common (and trickiest) combination I deal with. One person wants to build assets; the other wants to build experiences. One person is focused on the future; the other lives in the now. One desires pleasure; the other values safety. If they can balance this, it's the definition of Financial Happiness. Depending on which Money Why is dominant or how well-balanced they are, this can either be a great financial relationship or a disastrous one. Many times, I end up being the referee:

> FOMO: "Let's budget for renting a big beach house next year!"
> FORO: "What do you mean a beach house? We can't afford that!"

How do I tell which person is the FOMO, which is the FORO, and who is dominant? You guessed it—I ask those same three questions:

- How long do you typically keep your cars?

- Do you pay off your credit card balances each month?

- How long have you had your house?

In this relationship, each half of the couple gives a different answer. One person may keep their car at least ten years, while the other leases a new one every three. This type of couple also usually has separate credit cards, with one paying off the balance each month while the other carries a balance. This is not necessarily bad. In fact, having separate accounts helps minimize spending arguments in this type of relationship. As for the house, one person is usually happy with staying put while the other wants to move but is willing to compromise by renovating.

The FORO half of this couple has definitely been saving. How close they are to their retirement goals depends on how dominant the FORO is. Even if this person is very strong, it's unusual for the couple to be on track. I almost always need to adjust some things. Once I explain what needs to happen so they can retire, travel, and do everything the FOMO desires, they'll usually get on the same page. I'm not saying this is a single meeting; it takes a lot of negotiation and several go-rounds. Many of the couples in this category tell me they wouldn't even be having these discussions if it wasn't for me, which is extremely gratifying.

Not all FOMO—FOROs live happily ever after, though. The scenario I've been describing involves your average middle-of-the-road FOMO—FORO. The outcome can be quite different if one or both people in the relationship are at the extremes of their Money Whys. For example, an extreme FOMO (Happy Shopper) matched with an extreme saver (Miser) will frequently fight about money or stop talking about it entirely.

In situations like this, the FOMO is usually hiding their spending. When I tell a couple like this how much they're spending, the first one to look down knows the truth. In a very tiny voice I'll hear, "That seems about right." Meanwhile, the other will be shocked. Although they knew their partner was a spender, they didn't realize to what extent. This is a delicate time. The saver must be compassionate toward the spender. If they can no longer listen to one another because each thinks the other is unreasonable, then they've entered the danger zone for divorce.

SURVEY *SAYS* — FINANCIAL INFIDELITY: ARE YOU GUILTY?*

42% of US adults who are married or living with a partner say they've kept a financial secret from their lover.

28% of these adults say that keeping financial secrets is as bad as physical cheating.

7% say it's worse than a physical affair.

19% report having a secret savings account.

18% have a hidden credit card.

17% have an undisclosed checking account.

37% say their financial secrets are driven by desires for privacy or to control their own finances.

33% say they never felt the need to share or that the topic never came up.

28% say they were embarrassed by their actions, so they kept quiet.

17% say they were worried the relationship might end poorly if they confessed.

14% say they don't trust their partner with money.

11% say they don't want to divulge a drinking, drug, or gambling addiction.

*From a 2023 Bankrate online survey of 2,233 Americans aged 18 and older[38]

Handling a FOMO

DON'T

If you're married to a FOMO (or a friend, parent, or advisor to one), the natural tendency is to try to change their behavior by telling them to stop spending so much. But as we've learned, that's like trying to tell someone who's struggling to lose weight to stop eating so much. You'll never solve such a deeply rooted emotional problem with orders, lectures, or even facts. Shaming and yelling also won't work. Telling a FOMO to stop spending so much is too vague a goal and can be easily ignored.

---

[38] "Survey: Younger Generations More Likely to Keep Financial Secrets from Partners," Bankrate, January 22, 2024, https://www.bankrate.com/credit-cards/news/financial-infidelity-survey/.

DO

Help them realize their Money Why—*why* they love buying things so much and why spending is more attractive than saving. Part of it is the shot of dopamine—the feel-good chemical they get from shopping. It's the antidote to the stress, fatigue, or sadness they may be feeling. And it's addictive. Another component is how they were raised and the financial role models they had. Help them end the blame and the shame.

Ask if it's okay if you have a little discussion about some financial things tomorrow at 6:00 p.m. Giving them advanced notice lets them prepare emotionally. A FOMO needs to prioritize, so it's important to find out what's important to them. I explain that very few people can have everything, but most people can have some things. If you had to choose, would it be a bigger house or a vacation every year? Name-brand clothing or an expensive car? Once priorities are known, estimate the money needed to achieve them. (A good financial advisor can help with this process.)

When a FOMO sees that not everything is being taken away, that things are just being moderated, it feels achievable. It's very important to have a solid plan to implement and track progress.

An important question to ask yourself in this process is this: What happens to the FOMO if you become incapacitated or pass away? If they're unwilling and/or unable to take care of the finances, you may want to consider creating a trust and having a trustee do that.

Handling a FORO

DON'T

Say the following:

- You're a cheapskate!

- I care about people; all you care about is your money!

- Money won't buy happiness!

- You're going to regret being so stingy!

I can't tell you how many times I've heard couples say these things to each other in my office. It's disrespectful and hurtful, and it won't change the behavior. That's because the FORO believes they're doing the right thing—and not just for themselves but for the entire family. They're being responsible. And the entire financial world reinforces their beliefs.

DO

Help them identify their Money Why. In most cases, it will come down to fear—fear of not having enough, fear of not being responsible, fear of not being financially secure.

FOROs respond very well to a detailed financial plan. They *love* reviewing it. They want to be the key participant. They like working through what-if scenarios. *So many what-if scenarios!* I know that when I have a FORO (or two FOROs) coming in for a meeting, we'll be spending a lot of time on the plan. I love it! But it takes a while to prove that they can take a yearly vacation and still have enough for retirement and healthcare. A FORO's worries run deep. They need a patient advisor who's willing to review their financial plan with them many times over.

MONEY DISCUSSION ICEBREAKERS

Our Money Whys can make it difficult to talk about finances. For couples, this can become corrosive. After infatuation comes obligation—to pay the bills in a timely fashion, to save for retirement, etc. This takes communication. A 2024 *New York Times* article ("Why Some People Don't Talk About Money with Their Partner") provides some useful tips for making these discussions easier:[39]

- Schedule a monthly "money date night."
- Start with "low-stakes decisions," such as your next vacation, rather than when or where you'd like to retire.
- Imagine you're a team. (Joint accounts promote teamwork and force conversations about money.)
- Think of financial conflict as solvable rather than perpetual.
- Conversation starters:
  - What are your top three financial goals?
  - What are your most painful and joyous memories about money?

---

39   Ann Carns, "Why Some People Don't Talk About Money with Their Partner," *New York Times*, June 28, 2024, https://www.nytimes.com/2024/06/28/your-money/finances-budget-relationships-partner.html#:~:text=Why%20is%20it%20so%20difficult,partner%20will%20hurt%20their%20relationship.

The Second Marriage

If you didn't talk about money in your first marriage, it's a good bet you're not going to talk about it in your second one. If you're thinking of getting remarried, I suggest you go to a CFP® professional. Many religions require couples to go through counseling before marriage so their religious practices don't cause a problem. Since money is the second-biggest reason for divorce, doesn't it make sense to get some financial counseling before tying the knot? New love, even the second time around, is exciting and fun. You want to sneak away on romantic getaways and go out for dinners. What you don't want to do is discuss your attitudes about debt and how much is in your 401(k).

In a second marriage, your runway to retirement is usually shorter. There's less time to make a course correction. This is important stuff. I know your guy or gal is wonderful, but how are you going to handle assuming their debt or paying for their kids' tuition? What if they refuse to save for retirement or even to sit down and discuss it with you? I am continually stunned that people in their forties, fifties, and sixties get remarried without ever knowing the other person's financial situation. This will create friction and an unhappy marriage. Believe me, I've seen it.

THE SECOND-MARRIAGE FINANCIAL COMPATIBILITY TEST

Sure, the guy or gal you're about to wed is terrific, but are the two of you financially compatible? This quiz will help you find out before you commit:

Begin by answering the following questions. Then ask your fiancé to take the quiz.

1. Describe your ideal retirement.
2. Do you have a specific plan for getting there? If so, what is it?
3. At what age do you want to retire? (Warning: If the answer is "I plan to keep working," they may not have been saving for retirement.)
4. How much annual income will you need after retirement?
5. Where will that money come from?
6. Do you have any debt?
7. What assets do you have?
8. Do you have any divorce obligations? Alimony? Child support?

Compare results. Any significant differences are red flags that should be discussed.

Three Things to Remember from This Chapter

1. There are three types of money marriages: FORO—FORO, FOMO—FOMO, and FOMO—FORO. Which one are you?

2. A full 42 percent of US adults confess to cheating financially on their spouse or partner.

3. If talking about money is difficult for you, try a monthly money date night.

125

PART III
THE SOLUTIONS

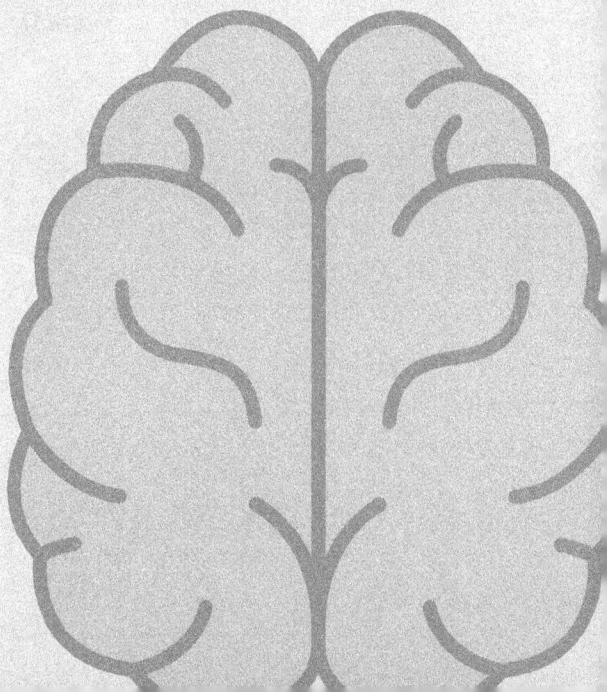

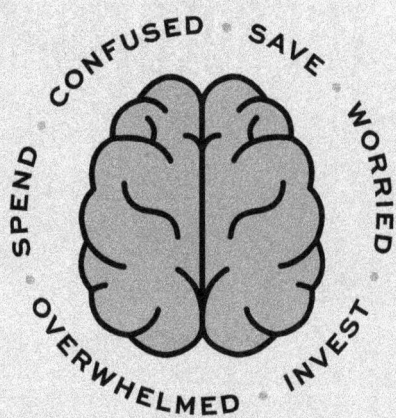

CHAPTER 9
CHANGING YOUR MONEY WHY

How many psychologists does it take to change a light bulb?
One, but the light bulb must really want to change.
—OLD JOKE

T he rest of this book is about achieving Financial Happiness. It's what everyone wants. Whether I'm giving a talk in the United States or the United Kingdom, whenever I ask how many people want Financial Happiness, every hand in the room shoots up. But what is Financial Happiness?

As a reminder, my definition, after much thought and talking with hundreds of clients, is this: *Financial Happiness is having enough money to purchase the things that create pleasure today while knowing that your financial future is safe.*

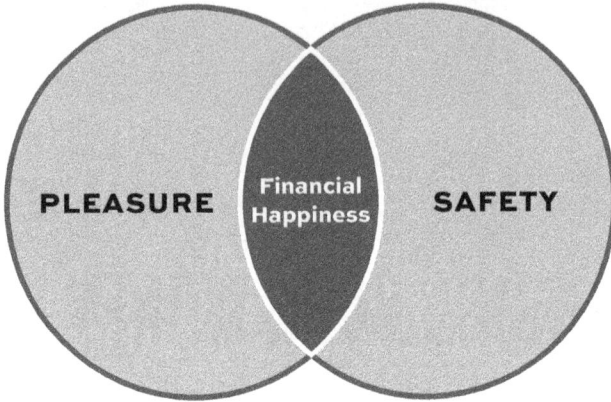

I believe you need two things to achieve Financial Happiness:

1. An understanding of your Money Why.

2. Access to professional financial advice.

By now you know your Money Why—what makes you tick financially and what drives your money decisions. This is a big step forward. Congratulations. But now I want you to consider the impact of those decisions. Have they created the financial life you desire, or have they created problems?

SURVEY SAYS

DO YOU WANT TO ACHIEVE FINANCIAL HAPPINESS?*

Yes = **100%**

No = **0%**

CHANGING YOUR MONEY WHY

WHICH OF THE FOLLOWING DO YOU FEEL IS CRITICAL FOR FINANCIAL HAPPINESS?*

Knowing I won't run out of money = **92%**

Knowing I'm on track for retirement = **65%**

Not feeling like I'm sacrificing today for tomorrow = **51%**

Having a plan for long-term care = **49%**

Knowing I'm creating multigenerational wealth = **30%**

(Results add to more than 100% because of allowance for multiple answers)

*From a 2024 survey of 212 clients conducted by
Evans Wealth Strategies

A few decades ago when my life was in turmoil, a friend gave me an audio version of the book *Change Your Thoughts, Change Your Life* by Wayne Dyer[40] and suggested I listen to it. One morning as I was driving to work, I heard this: "There is nothing either good or bad, but thinking makes it so." I hit the pause button and thought, *That is the dumbest thing I have ever heard in my entire life.* There *are* inherently good and bad things, and I certainly know the difference. Poverty is bad. Cancer is bad. Having your marriage break up is bad. I was so mad! I was mad at the author for being a crazy woo-woo nut job. I was mad at my friend for giving me such an incredibly stupid book. But for some weird reason, that line, which I later learned came from

---

40   Wayne Dyer, *Change Your Thoughts, Change Your Life* (Hay House, 2007).

Shakespeare's *Hamlet*,[41] stuck in my head like a bad pop song. After about a year, I thought, *Maybe there's something to this.* (I can be a slow learner.) *Maybe I can change the way I think about things and react to things, and together that will change my life.* And it did!

Being a left-brain nerd, the first thing I did was look for scientific proof that this was correct. But back then, not much was known about how the brain worked. Today, there's a truckload of data. With the development of the fMRI, neuroscience exploded. Researchers can now create a stimulus and see what part of the brain becomes active. They can show someone a photo of, say, the sale rack at Target and watch what neurons fire up.

A Bit of Brain Science

Back in chapter 4, you met your amygdala and your prefrontal cortex. Remember, these are the "feeling" and "thinking" parts of your brain, respectively—the two main regions involved in decision-making. In his book *Thinking, Fast and Slow*, psychologist Daniel Kahneman, who also won the Nobel Prize in Economics in 2002, calls them System 1 and System 2, respectively.

To see how these systems work, try solving Kahneman's famous bat-and-ball problem. A bat and a ball cost $1.10 total. The bat costs one dollar more than the ball. How much does the ball cost?

The answer that most likely sprang to mind is ten cents. That came from the feeling or intuitive part of your brain (System 1). And it's wrong! Take a second to do the math. If the ball costs ten cents and the bat is one dollar more than the ball, the bat would cost $1.10 and the total price would be $1.20.

---

41   "Famous Quotes," Royal Shakespeare Company, https://www.rsc.org.uk/hamlet/about-the-play/famous-quotes.

See your mistake? The correct answer is, the ball costs five cents and the bat costs (at a dollar more) $1.05, for a grand total of $1.10.

Here's what happened: Your impulsive System 1 took control of an apparently easy challenge and automatically answered using intuition. But it answered too fast.

When System 1 is faced with a situation it can't comprehend, it calls on System 2 to work out the problem. But, as Kahneman explains, your System 1 perceived the problem as simpler than it was and incorrectly assumed it could handle it.

The bat-and-ball problem exposes our tendency to take mental shortcuts. It requires a lot of energy to power the computer in our heads, so we naturally try to be as efficient as possible when using it. This is known as the Principle of Least Effort.[42] Checking the answer with System 2 would have used more energy, so why bother?

Taking shortcuts like this is unfortunate, because using System 2 is an important aspect of intelligence and informed decision-making. Research by Kahneman and others shows that practicing System 2 tasks such as focus and self-control leads to higher intelligence scores. By acting fast and relying on your amygdala (also known as the reptilian brain) instead of your prefrontal cortex (also called the executive function brain), you're not using your full intelligence and risk making poor or wrong decisions.[43]

It's not that one system is better than the other. You just need to be aware of how they can drive your responses and decisions.

Here's an example of using just our System 1 feeling brain:

---

42   "Principle of Least Effort," Wikipedia, https://en.wikipedia.org/wiki/
      Principle_of_least_effort.

43   Daniel Kahneman, *Thinking, Fast and Slow* (Farrar, Straus and Giroux, 2011).

THE PROCESS

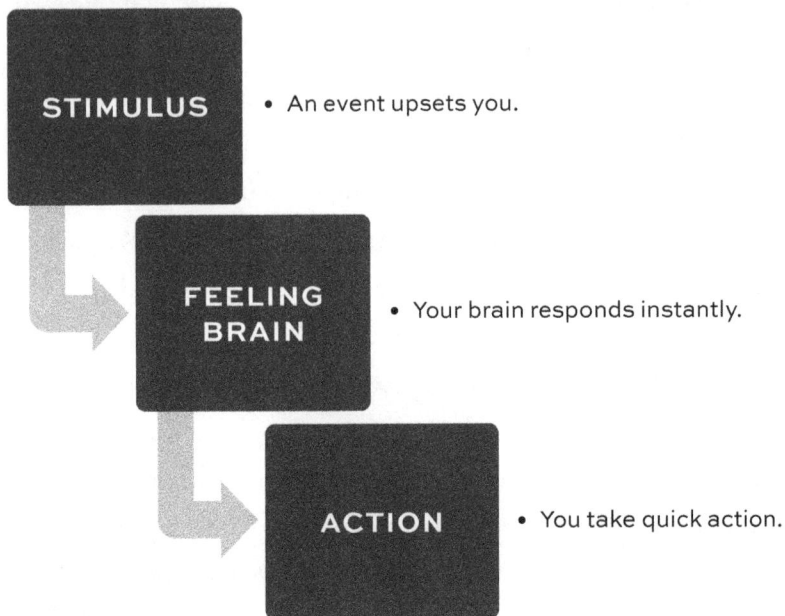

- STIMULUS — • An event upsets you.
- FEELING BRAIN — • Your brain responds instantly.
- ACTION — • You take quick action.

THE EXAMPLE

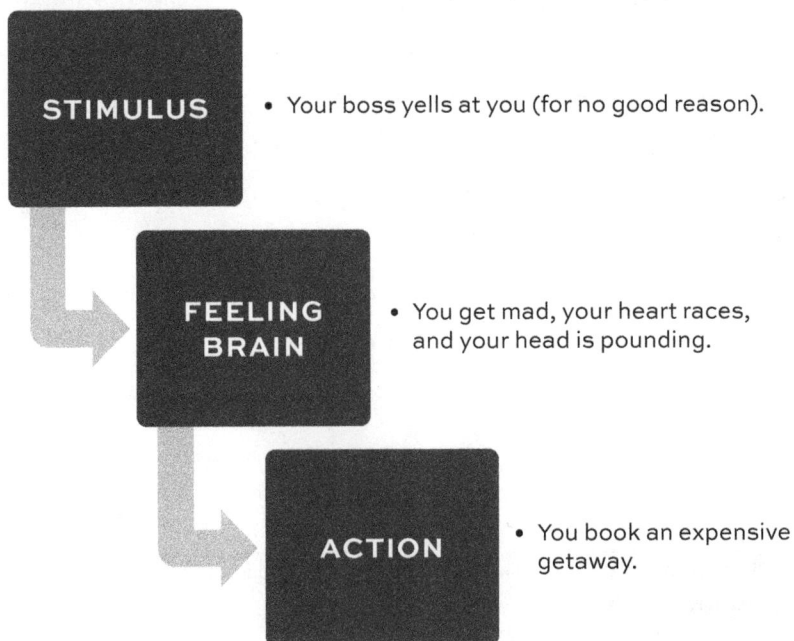

- STIMULUS — • Your boss yells at you (for no good reason).
- FEELING BRAIN — • You get mad, your heart races, and your head is pounding.
- ACTION — • You book an expensive getaway.

Here's the same example but with the System 2 thinking brain involved:

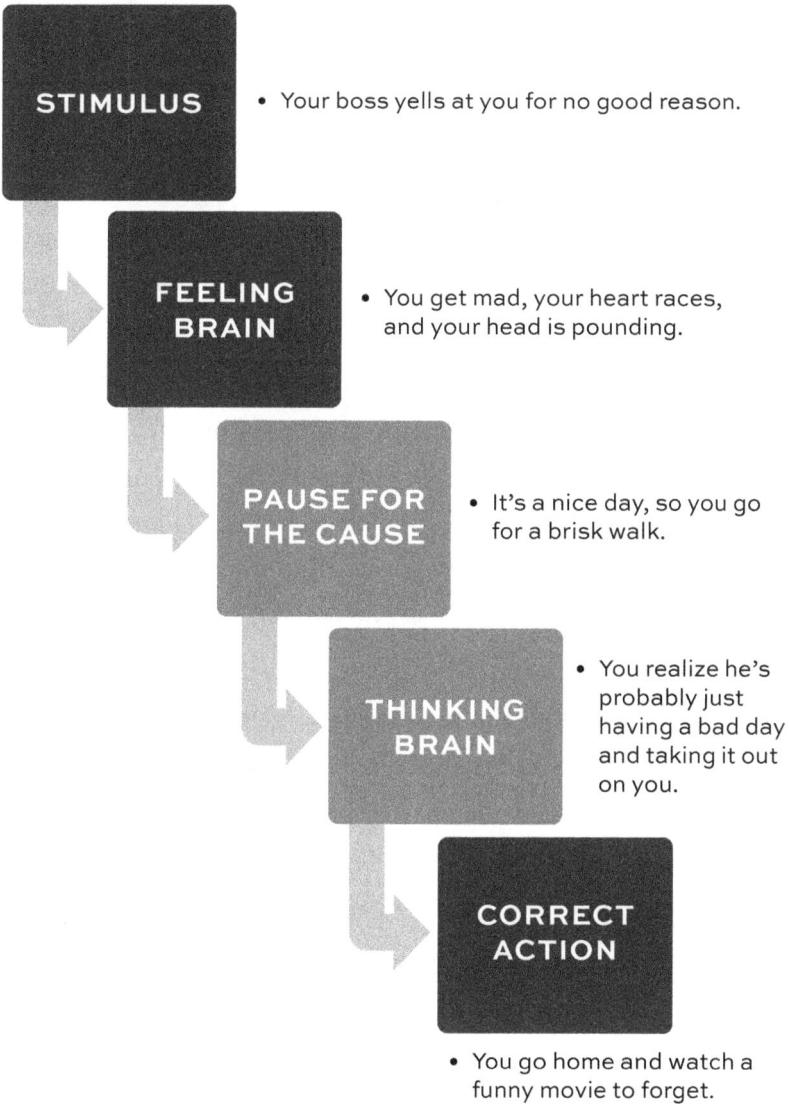

STIMULUS
- Your boss yells at you for no good reason.

FEELING BRAIN
- You get mad, your heart races, and your head is pounding.

PAUSE FOR THE CAUSE
- It's a nice day, so you go for a brisk walk.

THINKING BRAIN
- You realize he's probably just having a bad day and taking it out on you.

CORRECT ACTION
- You go home and watch a funny movie to forget.

Both examples feature the same stimulus. You were threatened, your amygdala kicked in, and your anxiety brought pain. But in the first instance, you relieved the pain by spending, while in the second you delayed the response and allowed your thinking brain to get involved, and the result was less problematic. This "pause for the cause" is key. You must allow time for System 2 to change the interpretation of the stimulus.

(ALMOST) PUNCHING AN ER DOC

Your Money Why is System 1 thinking. It's your amygdala or feeling/reptilian brain at work. Whether you're a FOMO or a FORO, a Happy Shopper or a Miser, you're making instinctive financial decisions based on your genetics plus the lessons you learned and the feedback you got, usually in childhood. In other words, you've been programmed to respond this way, and your decisions result from that.

If this is negatively impacting your relationships and/or your life—if you're mired in credit card debt and/or not saving for retirement, or if you have scads of money in the bank but no joy—you lack Financial Happiness and need to get System 2, your prefrontal cortex, more involved.

So, how do you go about changing something that's so innate? How do you change your Money Why? The first step is realizing that no Money Why is inherently good or bad. No Money Why is better or worse than another. So, if you've been blaming yourself for being an Ostrich or feeling embarrassed about your Eeyore tendencies, stop that. It's not your fault. It just is. You are who you are. But now that you're aware of your Money Why, you can begin loosening its grip on you. How do you do that? Let me tell you a personal story—one that isn't easy for me to relive.

After my son, Dan, collapsed and had his seizure in my office, I followed the ambulance to the emergency room. I was so upset; I don't even remember driving there. After he was admitted and his seizure had subsided, I was sitting by his bed. He'd dislocated his shoulder when he fell, and I was angry because he was in pain and it was taking forever for them to address it. Finally, the ER doc came in and got his shoulder back into place, and Dan seemed more comfortable. Then they took him for a brain scan. When he returned, he was conscious and looking better. *Maybe it was just some fluke thing*, I thought, *and he's going to be okay.* Then the ER doc came back and, very matter-of-factly and with no warning or compassion, told us that Dan had a brain tumor and that he was pretty sure it was cancer. Just like that. *Boom!* Our lives exploded.

The doctor left. No one came by to explain things further or to console us. I had never been so angry and so frightened in my life. I wanted to yell. I wanted to scream. I wanted to punch something or, better yet, that heartless ER doc if he ever returned. My amygdala was in complete control. My heart was racing, my breathing was shallow, and I couldn't think straight. In fact, I wasn't thinking at all.

Fortunately, I recognized what was happening in my brain, and I knew I had to stop it. Yelling at and punching people in the ER was not going to help my son. I wouldn't be able to make rational decisions in that reactive state of mind. So, I called upon a deep-breathing exercise I'd learned in a transcendental meditation class years ago and began settling myself.

What does all this have to do with changing your Money Why? It's an extreme example of the *stimulus* (Dan's diagnosis), my *feeling brain* (fight-or-flight response), and the *action* (my desire to start hitting people and throwing things). It took all the strength I had to breathe and engage my *thinking brain*, which immediately advised doing none of the above.

Poor financial decisions usually happen when the feeling brain is in charge. *Look at that! I'm going to buy it!* To end this, you need to lengthen the time between the stimulus and the action—pause for the cause. The longer you delay, the more your amygdala will settle down and the more your prefrontal cortex will take over. Remember that story I shared in an earlier chapter about my friend who wanted to buy the beautiful mirror? After convincing her to sleep on it, the urge subsided.

My go-to method for delaying action and helping my thinking brain take over is deep breathing. I inhale for a count of five, hold for two, exhale for eight, hold for two, and repeat this series at least eight times. I must have done this a hundred times those first few days in the hospital.

If this simple breathing method works for you, great. If not, there are lots of other methods for stretching out that vital time between stimulus and action, which I'll detail later in this chapter. I've tried many of them. Some work better than others depending on the situation. So, I have a whole purseful of tricks. Perhaps that's why people tell me how calm I always am. Little do they know. They don't see me when my amygdala is firing. (By the way, I still fantasize about finding that ER doc and sucker punching him. So, no method is perfect.)

Mind over Money

A stimulus doesn't have to be as traumatic as the one I experienced to trigger a response. And I hope none of you ever have to go through what I did. But people across the country get bad news every day:

- Someone picks on your grandson and makes him cry.

- You have a fight with your spouse/partner.

- Somebody makes a rude comment on social media about you.

- You don't get the promotion you worked so hard for.

- You get laid off.

We receive hundreds of stimuli every day that jump-start our feeling brain. Often when this happens, we feel pain. Do not minimize or dismiss your hurt by comparing it to my hurt (or anyone else's). Although the pain of my son's diagnosis and death was extremely profound, I also feel other types of hurt daily. It can be as simple as putting on a pair of pants that I swear fit me the day before and then beating myself up about eating too much. Or it can stem from meeting or talking to someone my age who's more beautiful, fit, popular, successful … you name it. (We all know *that* person.)

The feeling part of our brain wants to end or avoid all pain very quickly. Why not just go shopping for a great new pair of pants, ideally in slimming black?

But if we manage to turn on our thinking brain, it will tell us to go on a diet or start exercising more. Something that makes more sense and has more long-term impact. The hurt may remain, but it's not as intense.

Don't get me wrong—I'm not against buying new clothes or otherwise rewarding yourself when you're feeling down. I just don't want you to do it on impulse, especially if you can't afford it. My clients are afraid to tell me when they spend money. But I tell them, "I *want* you to spend money. That's what makes the economy thrive. I just don't want you to spend money you don't have."

Although I've been talking about the action of spending money to salve a hurtful situation, many times the action is *saving* money. For example, when I was laid off from the publishing firm and I had no idea what I was going to do, the first thing I did was count my money. I didn't count it once. I didn't count it twice. I counted it repeatedly. Doing so reassured me that I'd gotten a good severance and that I was close to being able to retire. For years, I hardly spent a dime on anything. Counting was my go-to, my comfort, my pain reliever. And I won't lie—it also made me feel a little superior. Look how good I am! (I always assumed long-distance runners felt this way as well. It probably isn't true, but it's what's in my head.)

I'm not suggesting we lobotomize our feeling brain. It's been around for centuries for a reason. If you see a tiger, run. If you see someone crying, put your arm around them. If you realize that a young man has brain cancer, break it to him gently. I'm simply suggesting being aware of what's happening and delaying the action to avoid making poor decisions.

Here's a story about a stressful morning at work when I (fortunately) did exactly that ...

FONT-ASTIC!

One of the companies I worked for had several large bank loans. As the vice president of finance, I was responsible for periodically submitting a report to the banks detailing the state of our business. I'd done it many times, and it wasn't a big deal. But the company had recently hired a new CFO, my supervisor. She called me one morning after I'd sent her the report and said, "This isn't right."

"I'm sorry," I replied, surprised. "What's incorrect?"

"It's the font," she said. "I don't like it. Can you change it?"

I dutifully revised the report (I think I used Helvetica) and sent it back to her.

The phone rang a few minutes later.

"I don't like this one either, Mary. Can we try Cambria?"

Well, you can imagine my reaction. *These banks don't give a damn about fonts! I'm the VP of finance, not some secretary.* Oh, I got myself all worked up. I was more lathered up than a model in a Head &

Shoulders commercial. But after a while it dawned on me: *Do you know how much I'm getting paid per hour to change fonts? This is awesome!*

"There is nothing either good or bad, but thinking makes it so."

Worry and Rumination

I've been talking a lot about how the feeling brain can throw us for a loop when it responds to a stimulus. The feeling brain is our alarm system. And when fully engaged, logic is useless. When someone's amygdala has been hijacked, this is *not* the time to tell them to just calm down.

But the thinking brain can cause problems, too. That's because the thinking brain, for all its valued rationality, is also the center for worry and rumination. While the amygdala operates and responds quickly, the prefrontal cortex deals in thoughts and language. It can dwell on a possible negative outcome and replay it repeatedly, despite no evidence of reality. The amygdala is still the panic button. But the prefrontal cortex can and will send danger signals that ultimately push it.[44]

For example, Bob reads an article on the rising cost of college and that it's expected to keep climbing. Although his children are four and six years old, he starts obsessing over this. He calculates what it will cost when they're college age. He looks at his savings. Even though this expense is way down the road and a lot of things can happen, he *thinks* he's in trouble. His prefrontal cortex then lets his amygdala know, and he panics. Not yelling-and-punching-things panic, but a quiet, simmering alarm. He tells his wife that all unnecessary spending must stop. No more date nights. No new cars. Renovating the basement is out of the question.

---

44 Kahneman, *Thinking, Fast and Slow.*

This is an example of cognitive fusion, which means Bob is confusing his thoughts with reality.[45] If this was an Olympic sport, I'd take the gold. I do it all the time. One of the best coping methods I've found comes from the spiritual innovator Byron Kathleen Mitchell, better known as Byron Katie. She developed a brilliantly simple way (called "The Work") of assessing stressful thoughts like Bob's. After identifying the thought, ask yourself these four questions:

1. Is it true?

2. Can you absolutely know it's true?

3. How do you react when you believe that thought?

4. Who would you be without the thought?[46]

If Bob took the time to do this, he might say his conclusion (can't afford college) is true. When asked if he absolutely knows it's true, he'd probably pause and realize that he can't be 100 percent sure. He hasn't consulted a financial advisor; he doesn't know what the future holds or even if his kids will want to go to college. He knows that when he believes this thought, he's anxiety ridden and tense. Without the thought, he's relaxed, looking forward to date night, drawing up plans for the basement—but still regularly stashing away some bucks for tuition.

---

45   "Relationship Between Cognitive Fusion, Experiential Avoidance, and Obsessive-Compulsive Symptoms in Patients with OCD," National Institutes of Health, April 12, 2021, https://www.ncbi.nlm.nih.gov/pmc/articles/PMC8072044/.

46   "Four Liberating Questions," The Work of Byron Katie, https://thework.com/2017/10/four-liberating-questions/.

MORE WAYS TO PAUSE FOR THE CAUSE

HALT Yourself

Alcoholics Anonymous suggests its members use the acronym HALT to pause when they're tempted to have a drink. It stands for hungry, angry, lonely, tired. The next time you're about to make a significant financial decision, ask yourself why you're doing it. Are any of these emotions driving it? Self-awareness is the first step to self-control. In fact, I'm thinking of getting a tattoo that says, "If hunger isn't the problem, food isn't the answer."

Break Old Habits

The more you do something, the more automatic it becomes. For example, let's say you're a high school teacher. When the bell rings at 3:00 p.m. and it has been a particularly hard day, your standard action may be to go shopping. It takes your mind off things, it eases the pain, and by the time you get home an hour or two later, you feel better. The problem with this behavior is that you're wasting money, and you're almost out of closet space. To change, break the habit. Instead of heading to Marshalls, try listening to a comedy podcast on the drive home. At first, this is going to feel stupid because your reptilian brain is in charge and wants its usual dose of "feel-good" action. *Buy something!* But if you pause and remind yourself that one more cashmere sweater isn't really in your best long-term interest, if you turn on a Sebastian Maniscalco or Nate Bargatze stand-up routine, the urge will pass.

Build Your EIQ

Psychologist and author Daniel Goleman coined the term *emotional intelligence*. It's a skill that allows you to recognize and manage your feelings without being controlled by them. The first step is being able to name your emotions. Once you can do this, you'll be able to identify what's behind them.[47]

Say your spouse/partner wants to go to Paris. It's been her dream ever since she was a little girl. Every year when you have the where-should-we-go-for-vacation discussion, she suggests it. And every year you say it's not in the budget, and it turns into an argument. You can continue dismissing her (and risking your marriage), or you can ask yourself, "Why am I denying her dream?" Is it because you think she's frivolous with money? Is it because you feel she doesn't respect all the hard work you've put into building a nest egg? By slowing down the process and separating the stimulus (her asking) from the action (your denying), you'll gain more insight into your reasoning and more empathy for hers. (She's probably thinking, *This is my money too!* and that you're being unfair.) Your emotional intelligence grows, and you'll start thinking more rationally about the situation.

Talk to Yourself

Inner dialogue plays a key role in developing emotional intelligence. What you tell yourself about a stressful situation will drive your actions. I like to say that you don't want to get all your exercise from jumping to conclusions. This is where it pays to get very curious if someone is being unkind or unfair to you. Rather than just concentrating on how it feels to you, turn this around in your mind and try to figure out what they're feeling and thinking. Chances are, it's not about you. More likely it has something to do with what's going on in their own life.

---

47   Daniel Goleman, *Emotional Intelligence* (Bantam Books, 1995), www.danielgoleman. info.

Monitor HR

And no, I'm not talking about those cagey individuals in human resources. Rather, I'm suggesting you monitor your heart rate. I have an Apple Watch that measures my heart rate—all I have to do is open the heart rate monitor app and place my finger on the digital crown to get my pulse. If it's higher than normal (an adult's resting heart rate is generally between sixty and a hundred beats per minute), I know this probably isn't the best time to tell the contractor to break ground for the new pool. Don't have a smartwatch? Just rest a couple of fingers on your wrist or neck and count your pulse.

Control the Chatter

One of the best books I've read lately is *Chatter: The Voice in Our Head, Why It Matters, and How to Harness It*, by psychologist and neuroscientist Ethan Kross. He says human beings talk to themselves all the time, and that's generally healthy. It helps us process what's happening, learn from the past, and plan. But sometimes it can turn into a loop of negative self-talk or "chatter." This is why, in chapters 6 and 7, I included a "Voices in the Head" section for each Money Why. This is the "worry loop" that takes over when different Money Whys face different situations. Fortunately, you can learn to quiet this chatter and engage your thinking brain. Here are some of Kross's tips:[48]

- *Take a temporal hike:* One reason we enjoy vacations so much is that they distance us from all the hassles of daily life. That's why they're called "getaways." For a week or two, we forget, gain perspective, and refresh. If you can't take a physical vacation, try a "temporal" or mental one. Go for a hike in the woods or a walk in the park, or play with your grandkids.

---

48   Ethan Kross, *Chatter: The Voice in Our Head, Why It Matters, and How to Harness It* (Crown, 2021).

By engaging with the outside world, you'll disengage from your inner world. You'll activate your thinking brain and gain perspective. Every morning, I get up, make myself a cup of tea, and watch the sunrise. It helps center me for the day. After my son passed away, I started going to the beach more often. I'd walk for miles and miles listening to the beautiful sound of the ocean and birds. I would look at the vastness of the sea and realize how insignificant my problems were.

- *Imagine yourself ten years from now:* Look back on the decision or situation you're facing as if from the future. Zoom in, and there's confusion. Zoom out, and there's clarity. Maybe this isn't such a big deal after all.

- *Create an imaginary movie:* Relive whatever happened as if it were a TikTok video. But put someone else in your role. Kross says this will lower your stress and delay your emotional response. (I like to have Jennifer Aniston play me.)

- *Lecture yourself:* Address yourself as if you were someone else, either by name or as a third party. Kross found that this strategy quickly decreases emotional turmoil. For example, when I got to worrying about writing this book and hitting my deadlines, I'd say, "Come on, Mary, you've been wanting to do this for fifteen years, and now is your time. Just sit down in front of that computer and do it!" This approach works better than saying, "I don't know why I decided to do this book. I don't think I can get it done. I have too many other things to do." (If you're reading this book, I guess it worked!)

- *Enlist an FBI hostage negotiator:* Well, not exactly. But you want to talk to someone who has that mentality and can show empathy and support but still reach a solution. Too often, when we tell our woes to friends and family, they commiserate with us. Kross calls this "co-rumination," and it doesn't get us anywhere. In fact, since they'll tend to agree, it just riles us up more. He says it's better to find a friend who will listen but at the same time offer objective advice and solutions. You may need to find different people for different situations—a person who can help with family issues, say, or one who's a work mentor.

My Journey from FORO to FOMO

If you decide you need to change your Money Why, all these tips will help you do so by extending the time to action, recruiting your thinking brain, and shedding new light on whatever situation you're facing. I know. I used to be a FORO. But after Dan died, I realized that life is short and you never know what tomorrow will bring. I know that sounds terribly cliché, but the reason certain statements become clichés is that they're so true. I evolved into a mild FOMO. I went out and bought myself a vacation condo. I turned the basement in my existing home into a playroom for my grandkids. Spending money on these things wasn't easy for me, but I finally stopped my feeling brain from instantly saying no and let my thinking brain reason that *Hey! You're not getting any younger, you can afford these things, and—most important—you deserve them.* Although I occasionally relapse into FORO, I've gotten more comfortable with spending.

Now that we have the emotional side of this nailed down, let's turn to how you can find a good advisor who will help you build a plan that will put you on the road to Financial Happiness now and in retirement.

Three Things to Remember from This Chapter

1. It's worth repeating: Financial Happiness is having enough money to purchase the things that create pleasure today while knowing that your financial future is safe.

2. Self-awareness is the first step to self-control.

3. Don't get all your exercise from jumping to conclusions. Pause for the cause.

CHAPTER 10

HOW TO PICK A FINANCIAL ADVISOR

There is nothing which we receive with so much reluctance as advice.
—JOSEPH ADDISON

Y ou wouldn't take a vacation without a plan. You wouldn't build a house without a plan. If you're having a big wedding, you plan. Figuring out how to fund your retirement is no different. You can't just wing it (though millions do!). Although people see the value in working with travel agents, architects, and wedding planners, according to a recent Northwestern Mutual study, only 33 percent of Americans have a professional financial advisor.[49] You need someone to put together a retirement plan for you and hold you to it. Not someone who says they're a planner; someone who's been trained as a planner.

Your financial advisor should also respect you, understand you, and encourage you to have a balanced response to money—regardless

---

49   "The 2024 Planning & Progress Study," Northwestern Mutual, https://news.north-westernmutual.com/planning-and-progress-study-2024.

of whether you're a FOMO or FORO. This means that if the market nose-dives, your advisor will encourage you not to make any rash decisions; they'll help you realize that the market goes down every four to five years and then trends back up. So, you stay the course.

Here are the most common complaints I hear from new clients about their former financial advisor:

- I don't understand a word he's saying (most advisors are male).

- I feel like he's always talking down to us.

- I hate going to the meetings; it makes me feel like a failure.

- He only talks to my husband.

- We never hear from him unless he's selling something.

- He doesn't understand how important traveling is to us.

- He never listens; he just talks and talks.

Of course, these are all red flags. If you nodded your head to one or more of these statements, your current advisor probably isn't well suited to you.

If you want to find an advisor who will be your partner on the road to retirement, a good way to start is by talking to a Certified Financial Planner® professional. To earn this certification, the financial planner must have at least a bachelor's degree from an accredited university, complete eight masters-level classes, pass a six-hour, 170-question exam, and have four thousand to six thousand hours of professional experience. Maintaining the certification requires continuing education as well as abiding by a code of ethics and a standard of conduct.[50]

---

50 "The Standard of Excellence," CFP Board, https://www.cfp.net/why-cfp-certification/the-standard-of-excellence, and "Certified Financial Planning," Accounting.com, https://www.accounting.com/certifications/certified-financial-planner/#:~:text=CFPs%20need%20a%20bachelor's%20degree,hour%2C%20170%2Dquestion%20exam.

To give you an appreciation for just how comprehensive this certification is, here are the courses candidates must complete:

1. Estate planning: Property ownership, taxation, documents, and implementation strategies

2. Tax planning: Impact of tax-related decisions for individuals and businesses

3. Investment planning: Modern portfolio theory, risk reduction, debt and equity securities, and asset allocation strategies

4. General financial planning principles: Professional conduct and regulation, including ethical and legal conduct

5. Retirement savings and income planning

6. Financial plan development: Requires students to develop and deliver a full financial plan based on a case study

7. Insurance planning: Insurance products, including private- and public-sector forms of insurance

8. Psychology of financial planning: Identifying and responding to attitudes, behaviors, and situations impacting decision-making

Why I Became a CFP®

When I started in this industry, I knew I wanted to help people reach their financial goals. I knew this would involve building solid plans, creating and managing investment portfolios, and imparting trusted advice. My employer told me that I needed to get my "Series 7 exam." It required no college degree or experience. It was just a test to make sure I knew the rules and regulations of the securities industry. It took me about three months of study to pass this exam. It enabled me to sell all types of securities, including stocks, bonds, mutual funds, annuities, and options, to name a few. I was licensed with FINRA as a registered representative.

I thought I was ready to go. But my goal wasn't to sell people securities. I wanted to help them identify and attain their financial objectives. Despite having a degree in finance and over twenty-five years in the corporate financial world, I knew I needed specialized training to do this. Just because you work in healthcare doesn't make you a doctor. The place I worked at wasn't helping me. They wanted me to sell, sell, sell. But I didn't want to be a salesperson; I wanted to be an *advisor* and *planner*. After extensive research, I discovered the CFP® certification. I loved it! It prepared me to do everything I wanted. I know there are other good certifications out there, but this one checked all my boxes. It was tough work to get the certification (it took me eighteen months), but you can't learn how to help people reach all their financial goals at a weekend conference at the Days Inn. It *should* be hard to qualify for that honor and trust.

SURVEY ★SAYS★

FINANCIAL BEHAVIORS AND BELIEFS OF AMERICANS WHO HAVE (AND DON'T HAVE) A FINANCIAL ADVISOR*

	WITH AN ADVISOR	WITHOUT AN ADVISOR
Have a long-term plan that factors for up-and-down economic cycles over time	79%	38%

Have an emergency fund	84%	48%
Feel financially secure	64%	29%
Have good clarity on how much they can afford now versus how much they need to save for later	79%	60%
Have taken a step to address the possibility of outliving life savings	83%	53%
Have a specific plan to pay off debt	79%	49%
Have inflation factored into financial plan	69%	48%
Have a plan to address healthcare costs in retirement	69%	38%
Will have enough to leave behind an inheritance or charitable gift	64%	33%

Data from the 2024 Planning & Progress Study, an annual research study from Northwestern Mutual[51]

What's in a Name?

Where do you get your financial advice?

- Banker

- Insurance agent

---

51 "The 2024 Planning & Progress Study," Northwestern Mutual, https://news.north-westernmutual.com/planning-and-progress-study-2024.

- Certified public accountant (CPA)

- Friend or relative

- Internet/social media

- Broker

- CFP®

In this crazy world, it's important to understand that a title is not the same as a certification or license. Queen Latifah is not Queen Elizabeth. The requirements for having a title range from rigorous to nothing. Some titles are just made up and used as marketing tools. Remember that FINRA lists 253 financial designations on its database, but *financial advisor, financial consultant, wealth manager,* and *financial planner*—four of the most common titles you'll encounter—aren't among them.[52] This means there are no standardized requirements (either legal or regulatory) for these titles and anyone can put them on their business cards. *Financial planner* is one of the most misrepresented titles in the industry.

Fortunately, it's easy to check an advisor's title and history. You have three great resources at hand:

- **FINRA Professional Designations database**: Although FINRA does not approve or endorse any professional designation, its professional designations database will explain what a title or acronym after someone's name really means. Simply type in the designation, and it'll tell you if any special training is involved and whether the issuing organization requires continuing education, takes complaints, or has a way for you

---

52   FINRA Professional Designations Database, https://www.finra.org/investors/professional-designations.

to confirm who holds the credential. Access the database at https://www.finra.org/investors/professional-designations.

- **FINRA's BrokerCheck**: This resource allows you to search an advisor by name and supplies a snapshot of their employment history, regulatory actions, and investment-related licensing information, arbitrations, and complaints. There is also a list of brokers who have been barred by FINRA. Visit https://brokercheck.finra.org to learn more.

- **CFP Board website**: To find and/or verify a CFP® certification, you can use the free searchable database on the CFP Board website (https://www.cfp.net). It'll also tell you if the person you're considering has a disciplinary history or declared bankruptcy within the last ten years.

Your Cheat Sheet

Don't hire the first financial advisor you come across or is recommended to you. Interview a bunch as you would for any hire. Remember, this person will work for *you*—at least the good ones will. So, how do you find a "good one"? Assess them in these four categories:

1. Competency
2. Honesty/ethics
3. Philosophy
4. Personality

If you're married or in a relationship, it's super important that you and your partner choose your financial advisor together, that you're both comfortable with this person, and that you participate in the planning (and review) meetings together.

If I were to write another book focusing on all the titles, designations, certifications, and accreditations in this industry, it would make *War and Peace* look like a pamphlet. Since no one wants to read ten thousand pages on this topic, I've simplified it for you. I'm going to give you a list of questions to ask when interviewing a potential advisor, and, unlike in school, I'm also going to give you the best answers. It doesn't get any easier than this. If the person you're interviewing hedges, says that's not important, or demeans you for asking, find another advisor.

Note that this is the investor-beware part of the process. You've most likely been told it's your job to know about stocks, bonds, alpha, beta … The reality is that your job is to find the right advisor. If you do your due diligence and hire the best person for your needs, you'll be able to outsource the rest. They'll handle all the nerd stuff. Only you know who is right for you. You can't outsource that. Make a thoughtful choice, because chances are you'll be with this advisor for life.

ASSESSING COMPETENCY

Q: What do all those letters after your name mean? (e.g., CFP®)
A: They stand for _____ (e.g., Certified Financial Planner®).

Q: Who awarded you this title?
A: The title is awarded by _____ (e.g., the CFP Board).

Q: How long did it take you to get this certification?
A: The average time to complete the course work and become certified is _____ (e.g., eighteen to twenty-four months for a CFP®).

Q: What type of training is required to get this certification?

A: It requires a _____ (e.g., bachelor's degree, CFP® course work that includes ethics training).

Q: What courses were you required to complete?

A: The courses include _____ (e.g., for a CFP®, see the list provided earlier in this chapter).

Q: Did you have to pass an exam?

A: I had to pass a _____ (e.g., six-hour exam administered by the CFP Board and score 75 percent or higher).

Q: How long have you been doing this?

A: I've been working with clients for _____ (e.g., CFP®s must have four thousand to six thousand hours of professional experience and must pass a background check).

Q: Is continuing education required to maintain this certification?

A: Yes, I must complete _____ (e.g., CFP®s need thirty hours of continuing education every two years, including an ethics course).

Q: Can I verify your status with a regulatory agency?

A: You can verify what I've just told you by _____ (e.g., CFP®s can be verified through the CFB Board website).

ASSESSING HONESTY/ETHICS

This is harder to judge than competency. Case in point: Bernie Madoff. Madoff had been the chairman of the NASDAQ stock exchange. He was smart. He was competent. His clients referred new clients to him—like most of us would, these new clients assumed that if their friend or sibling were happy with his services, then they'd be too. It was the perfect recipe for a Ponzi scheme.

Those in the industry had concerns, but there were no checks and balances. Madoff was the advisor, the broker, and the compliance department of his firm—he was even related to the accountant. These roles should always be separate. I know of one firm that refused to let him on its platform because he wouldn't supply audited financial statements or agree to a site inspection. The good news in this bad scenario is that it gives us some things to look for when assessing whether a financial advisor is trustworthy. Here are a few questions to ask (and the answers you want to hear):

Q: Who is the custodian of the money?
A: It should never be the advisor. The custodian and the advisor should be separate. For example, I am the advisor, but the financial services firm Raymond James is my custodian. All my trades go through them. They provide an entire system of checks and balances to keep me honest and your money safe. Madoff was the custodian of the money in his scheme. Big red flag.

Q: Who does your compliance?
A: Financial compliance is an ongoing process of making sure that an advisor or business is following all the relevant laws and regulations outlined by the financial regulatory bodies. An advisor should not be doing their own compliance. Raymond James does mine.

Q: Are you and your firm listed on BrokerCheck?
A: Even if they say they are, double-check.

Q: Does the certification you hold have an ethics standard?
A: You want an advisor who's had an ethics component to their training and gets ongoing training in this area. Basically, it's a strong reminder to not rip off little old ladies. If someone has ripped off

little old ladies (and been disciplined for it), this will show up on BrokerCheck (and also on a list of people going to hell).

Q: Are you a fiduciary?
A: I get this question from clients all the time, even though most people have no idea what it means. Being a fiduciary simply means that I am required to act in my clients' best interest, not mine. How is that determined? It depends on what is most appropriate for the client. When I'm working with someone in an advisory capacity, I'm required to work in their best interest when managing their account. Being a fiduciary is good, but not all clients need the ongoing services of an advisory relationship.

Q: Have you ever been fined?
A: Verify what the advisor tells you on BrokerCheck. Any disciplinary actions will appear there. But if the answer is yes, don't assume they're a bad character. Ask what happened. Sometimes there are miscommunications between advisors and clients.

Q: How many financial firms have you worked for?
A: It takes a lot of work to change firms, especially if they're in different states (licensing requirements differ). So, an advisor who has hopped around a lot may be problematic. Again, you can find this on BrokerCheck.

Most of the people in this industry are honest. There are very few Madoffs, but unfortunately, they're the ones who make the headlines and create fear. I wish some of the hardworking financial planners who are making people's lives better would get more recognition. The attention the crooks get can erode trust in the system and prevent people from seeking the advice they need.

ASSESSING PHILOSOPHY

Some advisors just want to sell investments (stocks, bonds, mutual funds) and investment products (annuities). Others want to only do planning. I believe you're best served by someone who does both.

Clients often ask me if an investment is good or bad. I tell them that most investments are neither. The question they should be asking is this: "Is this investment appropriate for me?" For example, stilettos are beautiful shoes. My young, skinny, gorgeous niece looks wonderful in them. For me—no way. I'd break my neck and develop bunions. If I don't know anything about you, I have no idea what's appropriate for you, and neither does anyone else. The only way for an advisor to determine what you need is to get to know you and your Money Why. Then they can help you develop a comprehensive financial plan.

Here are some important questions to ask (and the answers you should get) to be sure your money philosophy matches your advisor's:

Q: In this relationship, what are your responsibilities and what are mine?
A: This may seem like an odd question, but it's an important one. As far as I'm concerned, your role is to meet with me on a regular basis, update me on life changes, and ask me about anything you don't understand. My role is to meet with you regularly, answer your questions, build a portfolio suited to your unique needs, and provide solutions to get you where you want to be in your financial life.

Q: Are you independent?
A: In other words, do you own your firm, or do you work for someone else? An advisor doesn't need to be independent to be good, but I've always found independent advisors to have an ambitious, entrepreneurial spirit that I admire. I decided to open my own business because I wanted to abide by the highest moral standards and have the

freedom to provide investment options that were best for my clients. The financial firm I worked for previously didn't share my philosophy. (Note: An independent advisor still needs oversight—a custodian for the money.)

Q: (If they're not independent …) What firm do you work for, and are you limited in the investment options you can provide to me?
A: Some firms will tell their staff on Monday morning to push certain products, not for their clients' benefit but for their own. I was in such a position for a short time, and I couldn't handle being told to do that. Your advisor should be able to help you invest in anything. Here's an analogy: If you were throwing a dinner party, you could order everything from Domino's and hope everyone enjoys pizza, garlic knots, and indigestion. Or you could go to Trader Joe's and buy a variety of wholesome appetizers and entrees that would please everyone. Investing is similar. You want an advisor who can provide a wide selection of products that suit your taste.

Q: What impact do you think emotions have on financial decisions?
A: If their answer is none, run. A good financial advisor will realize that emotions play an enormous role in saving, spending, and investment decisions. The now popular field of behavioral finance has proven this point again and again. Bonus points if they've heard of it.

Q: How do you get paid (commission- or fee-based)?
A: If they're commission based, they make their money on transactions (buying and selling securities). If they're fee based, you'll be charged a percentage of your portfolio on a quarterly or annual basis. My philosophy is that I prosper when my clients prosper, and I suffer when they suffer. We're on the same side of the desk. So, I prefer working with clients in a fee-based advisory relationship when appropriate.

Q: (If fee-based ...) What other services do you provide?

A: You don't want someone who'll just work up a financial plan, build a portfolio, and then forget about you. You want someone who'll review your plan and portfolio annually and be there to answer the phone when you have a problem. At my office we have a list of fifty things we do for clients. Here's another analogy: A bicycle and a Lexus are both forms of transportation. The car costs fifty to a hundred times what the bike costs, but it's providing you with a lot more amenities. So, don't just look at the cost of financial services; look at the services.

Q: How is your staff compensated?

A: My staff is salaried. Whatever investment suggestions they make to clients, their compensation doesn't change. While this is not necessary, I feel this is reassuring to clients.

Q: What is your succession plan?

A: This is important, particularly if the advisor is independent. In other words, who will take over the business if something happens to the advisor or they retire? Ideally, they'll be looking to establish a legacy business rather than sell all or part of it to someone else. This is important, because the new owner may have an entirely different philosophy, and changing advisors is something most people dread.

In most firms, each advisor has the freedom to operate their part of the business as they see fit. I don't subscribe to that. There is no Mary way or Crystal way; there's the Evans Wealth Strategies way. We're not siloed; we are one team with the same philosophy, policies, procedures, and portfolios. I like to joke that we run the Starbucks model. Order a mocha locha (I don't know; I drink tea), and it will always be the same.

When I got my cancer diagnosis, Crystal filled in for me. Some of my clients told me they actually thought she was my daughter because we said the same things and thought the same way. I took that as a great compliment and reassurance. If something had happened to me, my clients would still have received the same attention and service.

ASSESSING PERSONALITY

At my office, we often say that we can't take a client who doesn't have a sense a humor. That's because—as you've probably realized by now—I do! And the people I hire do, too. Being able to laugh helps keep us sane. If a client lacks a sense of humor, they won't be entertained, and sooner or later we'll say something they won't be happy about.

Everyone in my office has a nickname. I'm the Professor. Crystal is the Popular Girl. And we also have the "A" Student and the Fun-Loving Nerd. Our stance is that we take what we do very seriously, but we don't take ourselves too seriously. We deal with money—a known cause of anxiety. If we can add a little humor to help you relax, that's awesome.

Money is inherently stressful—your advisor shouldn't make that stress worse.

Here are a few questions to ask the advisor and a few more to ask yourself (designated as "Q for U"). These will help you further gauge the advisor's personality and whether they care more about you or themselves. (Note that it might take a few meetings to see if your personalities jibe.)

Q: Where did you get that suit?
A: If they're in Armani and you're (trying) to rock the latest blazer from Target, well, their taste might be a bit different than yours.

Q: What's the funniest thing that happened to you lately?
A: If they stare at you like you're crazy and can't come up with anything, they probably take life too seriously. When I get asked this

question, I go on and on. Despite everything I've been through, I'm a happy optimist, and life is perpetually entertaining.

Q for U: What percentage of the meeting did you get to talk?
A: You should've had the floor for at least half the time you were together. A good advisor is a good listener.

Q for U: Was their first question about you, or did they tell you everything they've been doing lately?
A: This meeting should be all about you.

Q for U: Do you think you'll look forward to future meetings with this person?
A: If not, it's the wrong person.

Q for U: How did their office make you feel?
A: My goal is to put clients at ease, to make them feel comfortable. When I hold parties or events, they're always in my office because that's our home, and I want you to feel welcome there. When I see clients fixing themselves coffee or taking dirty dishes back to the kitchen, that makes me happy and tells me they're relaxed. That's the approach you need with money.

Q for U: Did they show you a lot of charts and graphs?
A: Remember, you're not one chart away from Financial Happiness. Money is emotional. Your advisor should be asking about your feelings, thoughts, and fears. (And maybe showing a few graphs—I do love graphs.)

Q for U: Did they demean, belittle, or make you feel guilty about not doing better financially?
A: If so, this is not the advisor for you.

Q for U: What does your gut tell you about this guy or gal?
A: All else being said, trust your gut.

Three Things to Remember from This Chapter

1. Only 33 percent of Americans have a professional financial advisor compared to 69 percent of millionaires who do.

2. A title is not the same as a certification.

3. Before hiring an advisor, gauge their competency, honesty/ethics, philosophy, and personality.

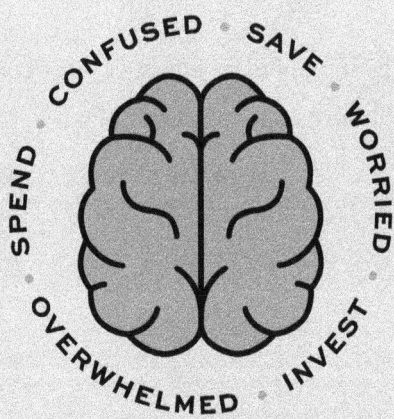

CHAPTER 11

YOUR PLAN FOR FINANCIAL HAPPINESS

Plans are nothing; planning is everything.
—DWIGHT D. EISENHOWER

Here is a plan for a house that my granddaughter drew when she was six:

Here is a plan for a house drawn by a professional architect:

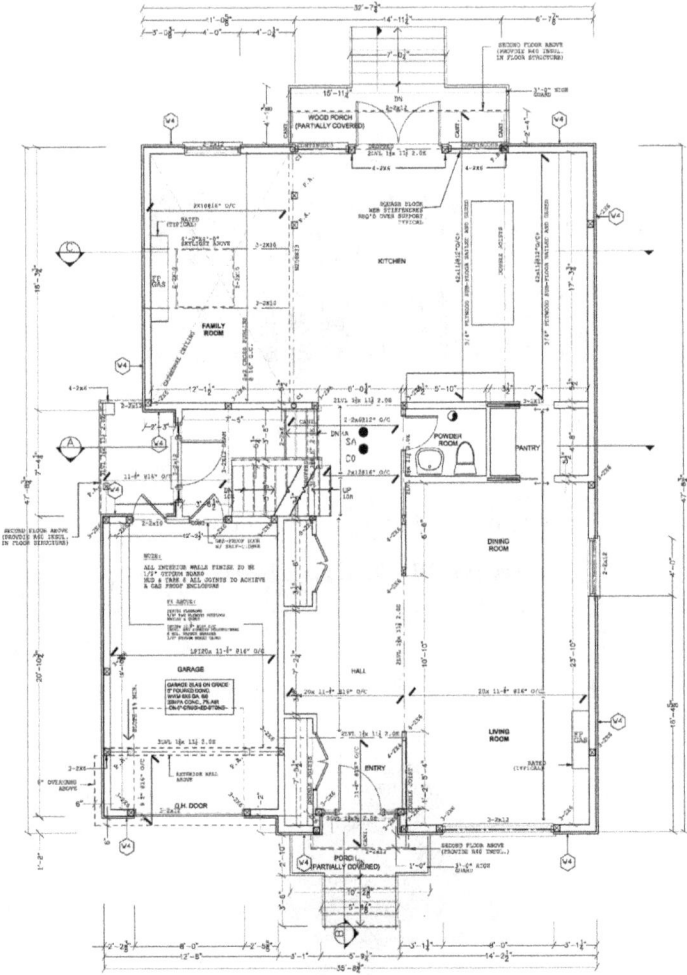

Which one would you like as the blueprint for your dream home? Although this might seem like a foolish question, you'd be amazed at what passes for financial plans these days. Sometimes they're built on the answers to just a few questions. That's like an architect asking, "Do you want a big house or a small house, and how many bedrooms do you want?" Then saying, "Okay, I got this. We'll get it built!"

For kicks, I did an internet search for "financial plans." All kinds of templates and tools popped up, suggesting this might be a DIY project I could tackle this weekend after regrouting the tub. The top result was an ad for an "AI-powered financial plan." Imagine that. I give all my information to a bot, and it spits back a financial plan in seconds. But there's one big problem with using online tools/templates to do it yourself or having artificial intelligence do it for you. As I've been hammering home in every chapter, money is emotional. It's more than just data. Neither AI nor some template is going to pick up on your emotions. Even though they represent cutting-edge technology, they're a throwback to the old way of financial planning and the belief that all you're missing is data, that you're one graph away from Financial Happiness. Don't be fooled by this. Plus, when a market or life crisis hits, who are you going to call to talk you off the cliff? A good financial planner will be there for you.

If someone isn't spending a few hours asking questions about your goals and desires, it's not a legitimate plan. And if you're not meeting annually to review and revise the plan, it's not as functional as it should be. As you've been learning, a financial plan isn't just about numbers. It's about dreams, hopes, and wishes. It's also about fears and anxieties. In other words, it's about emotions first and then the numbers. We are emotional creatures, and our feelings affect the development of, implementation of, and adherence to a financial plan.

Developing a financial plan is very similar to building a house. You don't start by going to Home Depot and picking out flooring and faucets. Instead, you decide what type of house you want (size, location, style …) and then assess whether you can afford it. If you're in a relationship, you and your partner figure this out together. The same thing should happen with a financial plan. You first decide on the type of retirement you want (lifestyle, location, spending …) and then whether you'll be able to afford it with your current level of saving. You and your partner should figure this out together. In this situation, your financial advisor becomes the architect of your plan.

True financial planning is fundamentally concerned with helping people reach their financial goals. It's the movement from fear to faith. But instead of assuming that everyone makes logical financial decisions, advisors should base their guidance on how people really think and act. Your Money Why is what drives your financial choices, and your long-term plan should take that into consideration.

Before I get into the specific components of a good plan, here are a few caveats:

- Hope is not a strategy or plan.

- Playing the lottery is not a strategy or plan.

- Prayer is calming, but it's not a plan.

In addition,
- procrastination is tragic,

- denial is disastrous, and

- greed is catastrophic.

The Eight Components of a Good Financial Plan

The following is the process I've developed over the years. I'm not saying it's the best way to build a financial plan; I'm just saying that it works for me and my clients. The advisor you've chosen may have a different approach, but if you picked the person based on the advice in the last chapter, you'll be fine. Just make sure they're hitting all these general points, and don't hesitate to ask questions if they're not.

A good financial plan is like an iceberg. You, the client, see just the tip (and are reassured that you're financially above water). But below the surface are all the details and hard work that went into building the plan and what's really keeping you afloat. The plans I draw up for my clients are typically sixty-plus pages, but since no one wants to read sixty-plus pages, we concentrate on a one- or two-page summary.

At the risk of mixing metaphors, it's like a duck on a pond. To someone on shore, the duck looks like it's floating peacefully along. But underneath the water, its little legs are paddling furiously. You're the duck: I'm the propulsion.

Okay, let's build you a plan …

1. MOTIVATION

I start every new client meeting with two questions: 1) "Why did you come to see me?" and 2) "What are you hoping to accomplish?" My goal is to get to know what motivates you. I intentionally do more listening than talking in this first session, encouraging people to be open about their money hopes and fears. In other words, I'm figuring out your Money Why(s). Here are some common concerns I hear:

- I'm not sure I'm doing the right things with my money.

- I'm afraid I'll never be able to retire.

- I'm scared I won't be able to help my kids with college costs.

- I'm terrified that if something happens to my husband, I won't know what to do.

- My wife was just diagnosed with early-onset dementia, and I'm scared.

- I just lost my job, and I don't know what I'm going to do.

- My husband just filed for divorce, and I don't know what to do.

- My mom just died, and I'm the executor. I don't know where to start.

I could go on and on. (I actually had one client admit he came to see me because his parents ordered him to, and he was fifty-two!) My point is that many financial planners assume they know their client's goals without ever asking. This type of conversation puts us on the same page. Whatever your challenges or motivation, I understand.

2. BACKGROUND STUFF

- When were you born?

- Where do you live?

- What do you do for work?

- Where do you work?

- What is your annual income?

- Do you have any kids or grandkids? If so, what are their
  - names,
  - ages, and
  - occupations (if applicable)?

- Are your parents still living? If so, what are their
  - names,
  - ages, and
  - current situation?

Without knowing basic information like this, I can't build a plan. I need to understand who you are and where you stand financially. A good architect will ask not only how many bedrooms you want but also how you plan to use them (master, kids, guest …). If the architect doesn't know that you're a grandparent, he won't design a kid-friendly space. He'll give you a house but not a home. One of my clients has sixteen grandchildren with another on the way. His financial plan is very different from that of a bachelor.

3. GOALS

Goals are different than motivation. Motivation gets you into my office (often with a grimace); goals help you leave my office (usually with confidence). In my practice, we call this stage "building your financial vision board." Over the years, I've found this to be a friendlier way to first determine someone's goals and then inspire them to reach them. It's the old refrigerator trick: sticking a photo to the fridge of the lakeside cabin you want to buy after you retire, the cruise ship you want to take through the Mediterranean, or the family and friends you want to spend more time with is a better way to stay focused on your dream than checking your 401(k) balance every month.

This is where your Money Why hits your Money Reality. I tell clients it's a little like going to a new doctor—you must answer a lot of questions. Ready?

- When do you want to retire or know that you *can* retire? (It's always easier going to work knowing you eventually won't have to.)

- Describe your retirement. Will you stay in your current home, or will you move? If you plan to move, where to? How will you spend your time?

- Are there any children or grandchildren you want to help educate?

- Do you like to travel? If so, how much do you typically spend on a vacation? Do you want to travel more frequently in retirement?

- How important is multigenerational wealth transfer to you?

- How important is charitable giving to you?

- Do you have a parent or any other adult who may become your financial dependent?

- Can you tell me, on a net basis, how much money you're living on now? (Pressure reliever: almost no one knows this number; we calculate it.)

- Is there anything else you're interested in that I failed to ask about?

As I learn people's goals, I ask them to sort their goals into needs, wants, and wishes. I get some interesting answers. One client insisted I establish a fund for her to buy shoes. I guess for her that's a need, and I must say she does have some dynamite shoes! I've also had more than one gentleman tell me he *needs* to golf four or five times a week. I quietly move some requests to the wants and wishes portion of the plan.

This is my favorite part of the financial planning process. Many times, if a married couple comes to see me, I realize they haven't discussed these things with each other before. It's fun to help them come together—or not. Your financial planner's list of questions may not be the same as mine, but it should cover these same general topics. And when I can help you fulfill all your needs with money to spare—that's a beautiful thing.

SURVEY *SAYS*

HOW DOES HAVING A FINANCIAL PLAN AFFECT YOUR ANXIETY ABOUT THE FUTURE?*

Reduces it a lot = **73%**

Reduces it somewhat = **25%**

No significant effect = **2%**

From a 2024 survey of 212 clients conducted by Evans Wealth Strategies

4. RESOURCES

Once you have established your goals and agreed to them, the next step is figuring out if you have the resources to fund your dreams. It continually amazes me how often I meet new prospects and they immediately hand me their financial documents. They're shocked that I want to get to know them and figure out their goals. They often say, "The last guy didn't ask me any of this." I think to myself, *Uh-huh, and that's why you're here.* A good financial planner will ask *lots* of questions. So, tell me more about the following:

- Your home: Approximate value? Mortgage? Loan details?

- Other property: Vacation homes? Rentals? Details?

- Your cars: Year, make, model? Loans or leases? How long do you typically keep your cars?

- Checking and savings accounts: Balances?

- Investment accounts: Types? Balances? Regular withdrawals or deposits?

- Retirement accounts: Types? Balances? Regular withdrawals or deposits?

- Pensions: Active or frozen? Do you know the payment amount at retirement? Withdrawal options upon retirement?

- Expected inheritance (normally, this is not a given and shouldn't be used as a guarantee, but I do note it).

- Other assets: Anything noteworthy?

Now tell me about your financial safety and security. Do you have the following:

- Life insurance?

- Disability insurance?

- Long-term healthcare insurance?

- A will?

- Medical directives?

- A power of attorney?

- A trusted contact?

It's not necessary to have all this information at the first meeting (although if you show up with an Excel spreadsheet, I'll hug you). We can always estimate things and revise later.

If your financial planner overlooks any of these points, don't be shy. Volunteer the information. And don't be embarrassed about admitting that, say, you haven't been saving for retirement or that you have a chronic health problem. The plan is only as good as the information you feed it.

Every now and then I get a client who wants to use an anticipated inheritance to fund their retirement. I politely suggest that I'm not the advisor for them. It's not that you can't count on those funds, but it's tricky. People often overlook the fact that Mom, Dad, or Aunt Ethel may need long-term healthcare at the end of life. That's an enormous expense. I've seen more than one inheritance evaporate that way. Or the benefactor could change their will. (When was the last time you visited, anyway?) Inheritance can be a resource, but who wants to build their dream retirement on a loved one dying?

5. MEETING JESUS

After I know your Money Why, retirement dreams, challenges, and resources, I'll let you know your progress to date. If I'm dealing with a couple of FOMOs who have been spending like Beyoncé and Jay-Z, this is the meet Jesus part of the process, as they realize they're nowhere near their goals. Conversely, if I have a couple of FOROs who have been saving their entire lives, this part can be very affirming. If I have a FOMO and a FORO, this is usually where the finger-pointing starts. This is why I developed the money marriage techniques.

But this is about progress, not perfection. It's the rare individual or couple who walks into my office and has been doing everything right. Most people have work to do.

The real objective of a financial plan is to determine if you can reach your goals and not outlive your money—to purchase all the things that create pleasure while keeping your financial future secure. The way I determine this is by forecasting the return your investments will provide over your lifetime. This figure is key. To increase accuracy, I run a "Monte Carlo simulation."[53] It's a probabilistic model that examines a thousand different scenarios and estimates how certain investment strategies might perform. Conservative portfolios might yield 5 percent, while aggressive portfolios could return more. Everybody wants to know their probability of running out of money, and this helps me ballpark it.

When you're watching a good quarterback, you think every pass is going to be caught, but that's not how it goes. A good coach assumes that some passes will be caught, some will be intercepted, and some will be dropped. A good advisor anticipates all the possibilities as well.

Beware the plan that doesn't mention any of this or assumes one fixed return for every day, week, month, and year that you're alive. I'm pretty sure that won't happen. This simulation lets you know in what percentage of those thousand scenarios you won't run out of money. Eighty percent is pretty good. Ninety percent is better. If you're 100 percent, you're probably not enjoying life, you adorable FOROs. If you're much below 80 percent, you need to make some changes, my lovable FOMOs.

Many advisors, including myself, use the following meters to illustrate these points. I love them. At a glance, they answer the burning question of whether you'll run out of money. For full effect, read the captions aloud in the voice of Goldilocks:

---

53   "Monte Carlo Method," Wikipedia, https://en.wikipedia.org/wiki/
      Monte_Carlo_method.

50%

PROBABILITY OF SUCCESS
BELOW CONFIDENCE ZONE

This meter is tooooo low (my FOMO friends).

98%

PROBABILITY OF SUCCESS
ABOVE CONFIDENCE ZONE

This meter is tooooo high (my FORO friends).

83%

PROBABILITY OF SUCCESS
IN CONFIDENCE ZONE

This meter is juuuuust right! You're planning for tomorrow and enjoying today.

(Disclaimer: The projections or other information generated by financial planning software regarding the likelihood of various investment outcomes are hypothetical in nature, do not reflect actual investment results, and are not guarantees of future results. Results may vary with each use and over time.)

I have many couples who are in the rightmost, crosshatched zone and ecstatic about it. I call them my overachievers. As long as they're enjoying life today, I'm all right with it. I just want to make sure they're financially happy.

While it's necessary for you to understand the investments that are driving the needles on these meters, you don't have to know every detail. That's my job. Look at it this way: My husband gives anesthesia in a hospital. Do you want him saying to you on the gurney, "I'm considering these six drugs; here are their densities and molecular weights. What do you think?" Or would you rather him just make the call based on his expertise and put you out for the surgery? No doubt it's the latter. There is such a thing as *too much information*, and the financial industry is certainly guilty of it. Trust your advisor to keep you informed and make the investment decisions.

6. STRATEGIES

When most people see the word *strategies* in a book about money, they think they're going to start reading about how to pick stocks or allocate assets in their portfolio. I'm not going to do that. There is no simple formula or one rule to follow. And I don't think that's where you should be spending your time and effort. It takes years, if not decades, to understand all the ins and outs of investing (despite what the internet may tell you). The good news is that you're the expert on *you*. Only you will know if you are comfortable spending less, saving more, or working longer. It's the advisor's job to figure out which portfolios will get you there safely.

Not many people's meters are pegged at 80 percent when I meet them. I must usually suggest things they can do to move it in the right direction. Fortunately, there are lots of options:

- *Retire later.* The longer you wait, the more time your money has to grow.

- *Live on less.* Big impact, but hard to do. What are you willing to give up?

- *Reallocate your portfolio for more growth.* If I can get you comfortable with the market, this is the easiest move.

- *Start saving more.* Either through an employer or with an advisor, get it socked away. There are many ways to do this, but make it automatic.

- *Work part time in retirement.* Reducing your initial withdrawal from Social Security and retirement accounts can really help.

- *Downsize.* This is a common idea, but in my experience it rarely works.

This is not a comprehensive list, but it should give you a few ideas. I'll keep suggesting scenarios until I find a viable one for the client. Each person and family is different. There is no one-size-fits-all solution.

A typical first meeting for me often includes someone handing me their statements and asking if they have the right investments (after apologizing for not doing a better job, of course). They're shocked when I don't even look at the statements. My focus from the beginning is on understanding who they are and where they want to be.

If you're not where you want or need to be, this can be an upsetting part of the process. A good advisor will work compassionately with you to figure things out. This may take several meetings. You may need time to discuss things and think about it. But that's okay. This is emotional. You *can* make progress.

Besides knowing your odds of not running out of money, it's also useful to know how much money you can safely withdraw each year of retirement. This number will change annually due to inflation, amended goals, and of course your portfolio growth (or decline). Some people prefer knowing this number because they can comprehend hard cash better than probabilities. But both provide a useful way to glimpse your future.

By the way, the annual amount you can safely withdraw from your savings is not 4 percent. Although we hear that all the time, Moses did not hand it down. It came from a rookie financial advisor, William Bengen, who published his research in the *Journal of Financial Planning* in 1994. It used historical data from 1926 to 1976, which included the Great Depression.[54] While it may have been true at the time, it's no longer relevant. The amount you withdraw should be based on the details of your plan, not some historical number.

7. HOMEWORK

Yes, there is homework. My clients leave the office with a list of things to do, and I follow up with a summary of the meeting and a to-do list via email the next day. If you owe us some decisions or information, we'll elbow you. We know you're busy, but we're your accountability partner:

- If you decided to increase your 401(k) contributions, we'll remind you.

- If you want to start making monthly deposits into an IRA, we'll remind you.

---

54 "William Bengen," Wikipedia, https://en.wikipedia.org/wiki/William_Bengen.

- If you need to send us more information to make the plan more accurate, we'll remind you.

- If you need to get us your tax return, we'll remind you.

8. WHAT-IFS

As Ben Franklin supposedly said, "If you fail to plan, you are planning to fail."[55] Your financial plan is a living document. After you've done your homework and I have an initial draft, we'll take this to DEFCON 2. I call this the "What Are You Afraid Of?" meeting. We test the plan for that darn rug puller! Here are some common concerns:

- Social Security gets reduced or eliminated.

- Someone passes away earlier than expected.

- Someone gets seriously ill, needing long-term care.

- Your pension decreases.

- Inflation is higher than planned.

But that rug puller guy is tricky. He keeps coming up with things we haven't planned on. Maybe your marriage falls apart, you lose your job, or a parent becomes a dependent. There are so many things that can and will happen. This is why the plan must be reviewed at least annually. As your life changes, your advisor should be there to help you find a solution and revise the plan. Remember a few chapters ago when I said that if you're worried and ruminating about something, don't go to someone who'll just agree that things are bad? Instead, go to someone who'll look at things objectively and find a solution. That's your advisor.

---

55 "Benjamin Franklin Quotes," Goodreads, https://www.goodreads.com/quotes/460142-if-you-fail-to-plan-you-are-planning-to-fail.

Why It's Never Too Late to Build a Plan

Whether you have a financial plan or not, stuff is going to happen. Don't get caught in the mental trap of thinking you should have done this ten years ago and didn't, so it's too late now. It's never too late to make things better. I can't always get people to where they'd like to be, but I can usually help them make progress.

Consider Lisa and Jim. They were in their late seventies when they came to see me. They'd never been to a financial planner before. I'm thinking, *It's a little late, no?* But they were worried. Were they doing the right things? Could they afford long-term healthcare if they needed it? They wanted to help their granddaughter but were afraid they couldn't afford it. I put all their information into a comprehensive plan. Turns out they were in great shape and could help their granddaughter. They were thrilled, but the biggest benefit for them was the increased confidence of having a plan. Knowing is always better than not knowing!

All of us should have started saving for retirement when we got our first job. Not many of us did. But that's okay. We don't drive looking in the rearview mirror because we're not going in that direction.

When I was a kid, there was a copy of the Serenity Prayer hanging in our living room: "God grant me the serenity to accept the things I cannot change, the courage to change the things I can, and the wisdom to know the difference."

At thirteen, I didn't get it, but I do now. (I've always been a bit light on the wisdom thing.) While you won't be able to change some elements of your plan, you will be able to change others. A financial advisor will help you identify what can change and summon the courage to act. And thank God for that!

Three Things to Remember
from This Chapter

1. True financial planning is the movement from fear to faith.

2. The components of a good financial plan are motivation, background stuff, goals, resources, meeting Jesus, strategies, homework, and what-ifs.

3. Now is better than never.

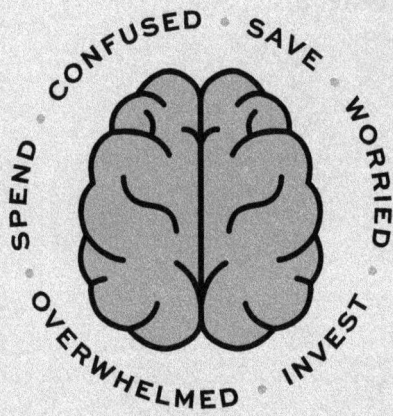

SPEND · CONFUSED · SAVE · WORRIED · INVEST · OVERWHELMED

CHAPTER 12
FROM FEAR TO FAITH

Everyone has a plan until they get punched in the face.

—MIKE TYSON

good plan expects the unexpected. When boarding an airplane, most people don't know or care who the pilot is—until something goes wrong. Then, while gripping the arm of the stranger next to you, you ask, "Who's flying this thing?" I bet the passengers on flight 1549 that landed on the Hudson River were happy that Sully Sullenberger was their captain. Likewise, I like to think I give my clients that same type of confidence when there's financial turbulence in their lives.

I started my business during the 2008–2009 financial crisis. Every day a client or friend lost their job. My phone rang off the hook. Unemployment rose to 9.9 percent,[56] home prices fell an average of

---

56 Gerald P. Dwyer, "Stock Prices in Financial Crisis," Federal Reserve Bank of Atlanta, September 2009, https://www.atlantafed.org/cenfis/publications/notesfromtheva ult/0909#:~:text=Much%20of%20the%20decline%20in,low%20on%20March%20 9%2C%202009.

20 percent,[57] and the S&P 500 dropped 48 percent over a six-month period.[58] If you weren't afraid, you just weren't paying attention. While many advisors go MIA at times like these, I viewed the crisis as an opportunity. I worked twelve-hour days and many weekends. *Do you want to know who's piloting your plane?* I am!

At times like these, a good financial advisor will listen and acknowledge your fears. They'll point out that similar things have happened in the past and tell you how long they lasted. But most importantly, they'll remind you that you have a plan, and a good plan expects the unexpected. Maybe it didn't anticipate this exact event at this exact time, but it assumed some turbulence. If any changes need to be made given the consequences, your advisor will handle them.

Since everyone was so scared in 2008–2009, I started doing client seminars. My favorite was "Why This Isn't a Depression." (The media kept predicting it would be, which didn't help.) I compared the economic conditions to those during the Great Depression. Attendees were shocked to learn that during the Great Depression, unemployment hit 24.9 percent,[59] the Dow closed 89 percent below its previous peak,[60] and there was no Federal Deposit Insurance Cor-

---

57   "Understanding the Effects of US Home Price Shocks on Household Consumption and Output," Federal Reserve Bank of Philadelphia, May 9, 2023, https://www.philadelphiafed.org/the-economy/banking-and-financial-markets/understanding-the-effects-of-us-home-price-shocks-on-household-consumption-and-output.

58   Robert Rich, "The Great Recession," Federal Reserve History, November 22, 2023, https://www.federalreservehistory.org/essays/great-recession-of-200709#:~:text=Real%20gross%20domestic%20product%20(GDP,10%20percent%20in%20October%202009.

59   "Labor Force Statistics," US Bureau of Labor Statistics, November 20, 2024, https://data.bls.gov/timeseries/LFU21000100&series_id=LFU22000100&from_year=1929&to_year=1939&periods_option=specific_periods&periods=Annual+Data.

60   Gary Richardson et al., "Stock Market Crash of 1929," Federal Reserve History, November 22, 2013, https://www.federalreservehistory.org/essays/stock-market-crash-of-1929.

poration (FDIC) to support the banks. (The FDIC and SEC weren't established until 1933 and 1934, respectively.[61])

I work very hard at helping people maintain perspective. Everyone likes to buy things on sale, except for stocks. However, there is so much emotion involved in investing that people tend to follow the herd. The trend is for people to buy when stocks are high and sell when they drop. Why? I believe it's because people don't have the perspective or confidence that the stock market will rebound. When I ask people what the stock market is, they often look perplexed. I remind them that it's just a bunch of companies and that when you buy stock, you're buying a small part (a share) of that company. I reassure them that no matter what happens in the world, the executives at these companies get up every morning and try to figure out how to make more money. Kellogg's decides to put frosting on the corn flakes—brilliant idea. Pizza Hut puts cheese inside the crust. Apple installs a professional-grade camera inside your iPhone. There are so many wonderful companies innovating every day. They innovate when the market is up and when it's down. They innovate no matter who gets elected to office. They innovate during times of growth and recession.

This gives my clients some much-needed perspective. Not panicking is a good thing. As Warren Buffett has said, "Be fearful when others are greedy, and … be greedy only when others are fearful."[62]

Turbulence is not always economic, though. Remember Y2K? September 11? The COVID-19 pandemic? Although these were

---

61   "The History of the FDIC," Federal Deposit Insurance Corporation, https://www.fdic. gov/90years/; "US Securities and Exchange Commission Mission," Securities and Exchange Commission, https://www.sec.gov/about/mission.

62   Warren Buffett, "Chairman's Letter—1989," Berkshire Hathaway "Chairman's Letter—1987," February 27, 1987, https://www.berkshirehathaway.com/letters/1986. html.

frightening and disruptive times, the world didn't end. We rebounded. The four most dangerous words in investing are *this time is different.*

With the right advice, you can handle personal turbulence, too. Divorce is a big fear factor, especially later in life ("gray divorce"). Someone may say they're relieved to finally be rid of the ogre, but in reality they're scared and often despondent. It's so easy to panic at times like these. I always explain that the panic is really coming from the unknowns, not the breakup of the marriage. My job as your financial advisor is to make those unknowns more known. For example, if your assets have been significantly reduced by the divorce, we'll rework your plan and see where you stand. Most likely your retirement goals have changed, too. Maybe you're finally free to do more traveling or go back to college and get that degree your ex always said was stupid. I'll build that into the plan. And maybe, just maybe, in the not-too-distant future you'll meet someone who is everything your ex was not. It's possible; I found love again at age fifty-six!

This chapter is all about reassurance, moving from the faith you have now because of your new financial plan, to the fear that will inevitably strike when something bad happens, to the faith that returns once you realize that you (and your plan) can adapt.

SURVEY SAYS — HOW OFTEN DO YOU WORRY ABOUT MONEY?*

Always = **17%**

Sometimes = **51%**

Rarely = **32%**

WHICH OF THE FOLLOWING, IF ANY, CAUSE YOU SIGNIFICANT WORRY?*

Running out of money in retirement = **58%**

Stock market will crash = **54%**

Inflation will continue = **47%**

I won't be able to afford healthcare = **37%**

I won't leave much to my kids = **20%**

I'll have to work into my seventies = **18%**

(Adds to more than 100% due to allowance for multiple answers)

From a 2024 survey of 212 clients conducted by Evans Wealth Strategies

---

Money Anonymous

I haven't mentioned this before, but I've been involved in the recovery community for decades—not as an addict (except for the chocolate thing) but as support for family and friends. My ex-husband was an alcoholic, and as I struggled to save him and our marriage, I started attending Al-Anon meetings. Al-Anon is a corollary program to Alcoholics Anonymous (AA), and it's designed to help the family and friends of alcoholics recover, too. One of the many things it taught me is that overcoming the bad stuff is always a multistage process. I got involved in other recovery programs and even ran a support group for five years. I saw many people use these step-by-step programs to overcome adversity and rebuild their lives.

One day it dawned on me: there should be a similar process for dealing with financial distress—a sort of Money Anonymous (MA) for surmounting money woes. (I've since learned there's a Spenders Anonymous and a Debtors Anonymous.) I devised my own plan based on what I'd been witnessing. With the important caveat that I am *not* a psychologist, here's what I came up with:

FIVE STEPS TO RECOVERY FROM FINANCIAL DISTRESS

Step 1: Shock/anger
Step 2: Fear
Step 3: Control
Step 4: Change
Step 5: Action

I believe the basic principles of recovery can be applied successfully to money. There are many similarities. For example, AA meetings end with the affirmation "It works if you work it, so work it." I could just as easily say that to clients who feel overwhelmed when something bad happens to them: "The plan works if you work it, so let's work it."

My goal with this chapter is not to be a Debbie Downer. I am a happy optimist (and I want you to be one too), but stuff happens. Whenever the rug puller shows up in my life, I use these five steps to react and recover. It works for me. I've seen it work for lots of other people. And I believe it can work for you.

Step 1: Shock/Anger

When you get laid off or receive a bad diagnosis, the common reaction is shock followed closely by anger. That's your amygdala kicking in.

But that's okay; you're human. When I'd meet someone in recovery who had just learned a loved one was an addict, I'd hug them and listen. In fact, I nicknamed our first meeting "the hug and listen." The first thing we all need when something bad happens is comfort and empathy. Our greatest desire isn't to be loved; it's to be understood. That's why support groups are so popular.

I do the same thing with my clients. Our first meeting after a disaster, whatever that might be, I hug and listen. You'd be amazed how much better that instantly makes people feel. I see the shock and anger start to subside, and I'm reminded of this quote from Mark Twain: "Anger is an acid that can do more harm to the vessel in which it is stored than to anything on which it is poured."[63]

Step 2: Fear

One of my favorite AA acronyms (and there are many) is FEAR = false evidence appearing real. This is so true. Whenever I feel fearful and my heart is racing, I remind myself of this. It's yet another way to pause for the cause and switch to System 2 thinking.

Some people get stuck in this phase, however—trapped in a cycle of regret that looks like this:

---

63 "Anger is an Acid," BrainyQuote, https://www.brainyquote.com/quotes/
mark_twain_120156.

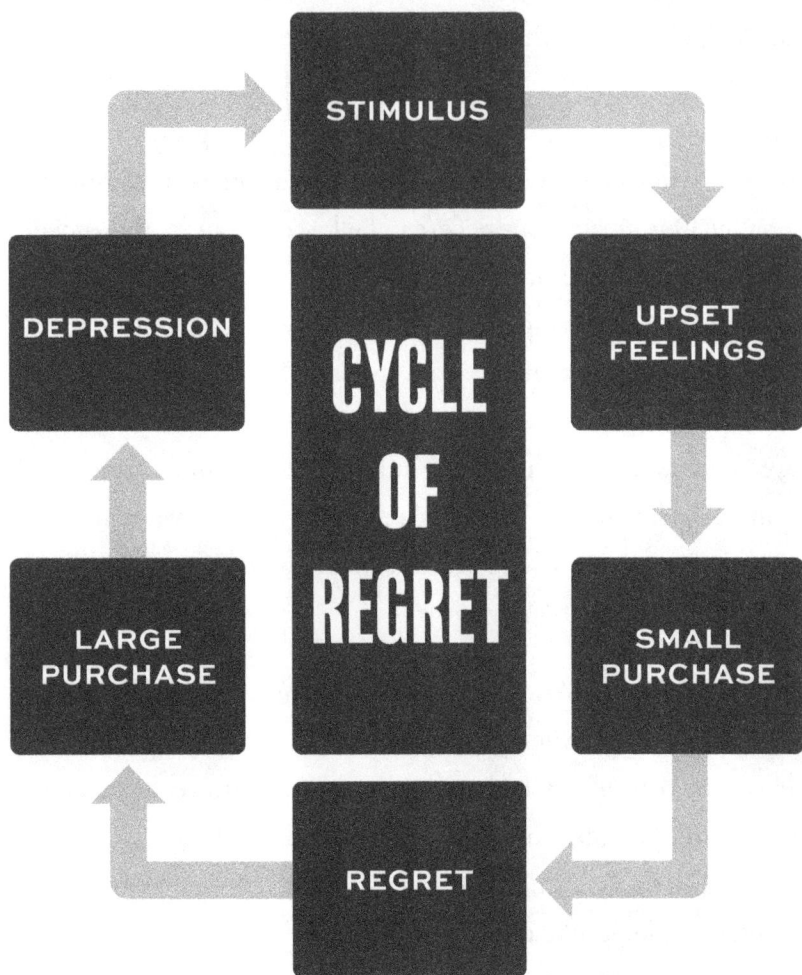

In this example, when something bad happens and emotion takes over, the person instinctively tries to find solace in a reassuring activity (in this case, shopping). But the purchase causes regret (*I can't afford that!*), which causes more emotional distress, which leads to a bigger purchase and eventually depression. Believe me, you don't want to get caught up in this destructive cycle.

Here's an ancient Chinese parable that perfectly encapsulates the antidote to catastrophizing and will help you avoid the cycle of regret. I probably think of it once a month:

Once upon a time, there was an old farmer who had worked his crops for many years.

One day his horse ran away. Upon hearing the news, his neighbors came to visit. "Such bad luck," they said empathetically. "You must be sad."

"We'll see," the farmer replied.

The next morning the horse returned, bringing with it two other wild horses.

"How wonderful!" the neighbors exclaimed. "Not only did your horse return, but you received two more. What great fortune you have!"

"We'll see," answered the farmer.

The following day, his son tried to ride one of the untamed horses, was thrown, and broke his leg. The neighbors again came to offer their sympathy on his misfortune.

"Now your son cannot help you with your farming," they said. "What terrible luck you have!"

"We'll see," replied the farmer.

The following week, military officials came to the village to conscript young men into the army. Seeing that the son's leg was broken, they passed him by. The neighbors congratulated the farmer on how well things had turned out. "Such great news. You must be so happy!"

The man smiled to himself.

"We'll see."

Step 3: Control

It's important to know what's within your power and what's not. Don't waste your time worrying and thinking about things you can't control. When you do that, you're directing all your brain power and energy away from what you *can* control.

Let's say you got laid off because your company was struggling. That was not in your power. What you do now *is* in your power. You put together a great résumé, you start networking, and you meet with your financial advisor to discuss how making withdrawals in the interim might affect your plan. Your panic subsides, and your confidence grows as you realize that the plan remains strong.

Likewise, everybody worries about a recession, especially when they're approaching retirement. But you have no control over whether this will happen or not. What you can control is having a plan for what to do if there is a recession. There's a distinction between planning for something and obsessing over it, though. Planning is examining the facts, figures, and historical trends and making informed decisions based on your Money Why. Obsessing is letting worry and rumination lead you to panic and distraction.

When you focus all your attention on what's in your power, your power grows.

Step 4: Change

No matter where you are in life or what has happened to you, the rest of your life is just unfolding. As author Chuck Palahniuk said, "The trick to forgetting the big picture is to look at everything close up."[64]

---

64 "Chuck Palahniuk—Quotes," Goodreads, https://www.goodreads.com/
quotes/561483-the-trick-to-forgetting-the-big-picture-is-to-look.

Walt Disney was in business for just a few years before the market crashed and the Great Depression hit.[65] General Foods, United Airlines, and Sony were all established in 1929.[66] Microsoft was founded in the wake of the 1973–1975 recession.[67] In fact, according to the British *Startups Magazine*, "Half of all the Fortune 500 companies were created in a crisis."[68] Where others saw despair, their leaders saw opportunity.

Don't waste your energy trying to figure out if something is fair or not. I've always assumed life is not fair. (Truthfully, as I've grown older, I'm not even sure what fair is.) Now I just deal with things as they happen. They are what they are. This is not fatalistic; it's opportunistic. For example, I started my business two weeks before Lehman Brothers collapsed. Everyone felt sorry for me. It was tempting to feel sorry for myself, but I knew that would kill my dream. When people are feeling sorry for themselves (as most Americans were back then), they need help. So, I stepped up and started providing it. It wasn't easy, but it turned out to be the catalyst for my new business, and we grew like crazy.

When the rug puller shows up (and he *will* show up), find something to pull you back from the what-ifs to the what-now. I like to hang out with my grandkids. Children are great teachers when it comes to keeping things in perspective and living in the present. If you're having a bad year, remember that if you live to ninety (and

65 "Disney History," Walt Disney Archives, https://d23.com/disney-history/.

66 "American Companies Established in 1929," Wikipedia, https://en.wikipedia.org/wiki/Category:American_companies_established_in_1929.

67 "Microsoft," Wikipedia, https://en.wikipedia.org/wiki/Microsoft#:~:text=Microsoft%20was%20founded%20by%20Bill,%2D1980s%2C%20followed%20by%20Windows.

68 Dannielle Haig, "Half of All the Fortune 500 Companies Were Created in a Crisis," *Startups Magazine*, https://startupsmagazine.co.uk/article-half-all-fortune-500-companies-were-created-crisis.

there's a good chance you will), that's only a little more than 1 percent of your life.

As the daughter of two Depression-era parents, wallowing was never an option in our house. I can still remember whining, "What am I going to do?" and hearing my parents say:

"Aim high—you're bound to hit something."

"There's always a solution—you just have to look hard enough."

"You gotta have joie de vivre." (No idea where my mother learned French.)

I realize not everyone has been raised to think this way, and that's not your parents' fault. Many people were raised to believe that worrying will prevent bad things from happening. But that's not the case. Worry and rumination distract you from finding solutions.

I'm not talking about ignoring the negative. I'm talking about looking for a positive that can come out of it. This is not the glass being half full or half empty. It's about the glass being in your hand. (Although I had a friend once who not only thought the glass was half empty but also spent a lot of time looking for the guy who stole the other half. He was *not* a very happy or successful individual.)

Step 5: Action

When I got laid off from my job at the publishing firm, I could've become a champion worrier. I was almost fifty years old. Who would ever hire me? My mother was dying from cancer, and I couldn't relocate. I could've spent my days fretting over my future, but I didn't. I had a great summer enjoying time with friends, and then I took action and got down to finding a job. From my perspective, losing a job wasn't that bad. Losing my mom to cancer was much worse. That spurred my restart.

Steve Jobs refused to hire people who didn't believe in themselves. Why? He knew he wanted to do great things, and he needed people who believed they could do great things, too. I look for that same quality in the people I hire. I want to do extraordinary work, and I want to make sure that everyone on my staff believes they can do extraordinary work.

You've probably heard about posttraumatic stress. It happens to veterans and victims of abuse as well as in many other situations. But did you ever hear of posttraumatic *growth*? It's the positive psychological change that some people experience after a life crisis or traumatic event. It's the old "What doesn't kill me makes me stronger."[69]

Some challenges can be handled on your own, like a job layoff. But others, like health problems, the death of a loved one, and divorce usually require help. It's not an admission of weakness to see a therapist or grief counselor. These compassionate folks have spent years studying the challenge you're facing, and they're ready to help. This is a worthy action. It's the same with financial planners. We've studied recessions and depressions and examined more charts and graphs than you can imagine. Seeking our help in a financial crisis is a worthy action, too.

I'll never forget the day a client called with the news that her husband had died during their vacation. It was a heart attack, and they were in another country. He was fifty-three. She was understandably beside herself. She was having a hard time getting his body back to the States. So why was she calling her financial advisor? I believe it was because she had gone through the initial shock-and-anger phase and was in the fear phase. She was trying to get to the what-do-I-do? control phase. This is a common response. Her world was crumbling.

---

69 Lorna Collier, "Growth After Trauma," American Psychological Association, November 2016, https://www.apa.org/monitor/2016/11/growth-trauma.

But the one thing she could do was take control of the financial ramifications. It gave her something to do.

I spent a lot of time on the hug and listen. (After hearing her story, I needed a hug, too.) Then, realizing that she needed to feel she was accomplishing something, I told her that she was entitled to the net present value of her husband's pension, which was almost $1 million. She was shocked again, but for good reason.

I was elated to bring her some peace of mind. We discussed how her husband would have been so happy that she was taken care of. He was such a good guy. We laughed and cried some more. She ended our call feeling better that at least the financial part of her life was under her control.

Over time, she recovered and changed her perspective. From crisis sprang opportunity. She told me she'd always wanted to buy a little camper and travel around the country. At this point in her life, she had the means to do so, and she eventually hit the road. She made it through the five steps and is a happy, contented woman. Not living the life she imagined, but still one that she enjoys.

Sometimes the Rug Puller Blesses You

I should point out that the rug puller doesn't always punch us in the face. Sometimes he shows up unexpectedly and gives us a big hug. If you have parents or grandparents who were raised in the 1930s, 1940s, and 1950s, you will probably be the beneficiary of the greatest saving generation. Because of the conditions they lived in, most were proud FOROs. When they pass away, so many of them leave an inheritance that shocks their descendants. Their frugal lifestyle belied their true finances.

I love it when clients tell me their parents or grandparents never bought new cars or furniture and used coupons for everything. "How

FROM FEAR TO FAITH

could they have all this money?" This is exactly why they have all this money! I always remind them that before they sell the house, look everywhere—and I mean *everywhere*—for hidden cash. Remember that your grandparents lived through the banks crashing and passed some of that fear, via love, to your parents.

After my mom died, my siblings and I went through every pocket of all her clothes. We were literally in her bedroom, pulling things out of her closet, and throwing five- and ten-dollar bills on the bed. (I really regret not taking a photo of that pile.) We also divvied up her furniture. My brother Bill got this nice wood table. It had a turntable built into it. Well, six months later, he called me and said, "It looks like I owe you money." He'd found four hundred-dollar bills in there! Despite all the stories I've shared about her reusing Reynolds Wrap and such, she still left us a sizable inheritance. Thanks, Mom.

Three Things to Remember from This Chapter

1. A good plan expects the unexpected.

2. The five stages for regaining faith are 1) shock/anger, 2) fear, 3) control, 4) perspective, and 5) action.

3. When you focus all your attention on what's in your power, your power grows.

201

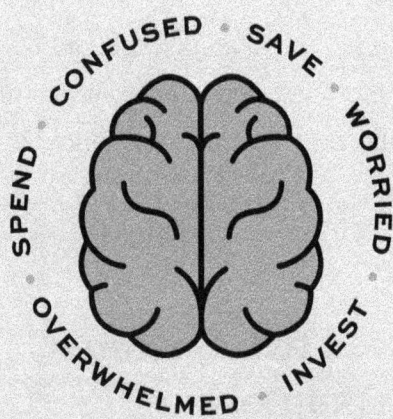

CHAPTER 13

THE BIG OPPORTUNITY

Skate to where the puck is going to be, not where it has been.
—WAYNE GRETZKY

Y ou now have everything you need to begin your journey toward Financial Happiness. I hope your dreams feel more within reach.

Writing this book is the culmination of a dream I've had for fifteen years. But my big dream is for this book to become a catalyst for change in the financial services industry. I want to see the industry redraw the line between what is their responsibility and what is the responsibility of the everyday investor. With the Big Sin, the burden of saving for retirement shifted to employees, and the need for professional financial planning grew. I think the industry can do more to meet this need. I like to call it the Big Opportunity.

I've just spent two hundred pages yakking about why money is emotional, how to figure out your Money Why, what to look for in a financial advisor, and how to build a financial plan that can adapt to any circumstance. But here's the thing: all that should *not* be your job. When you visit a doctor, accountant, or lawyer, there's no question they've been highly trained and meet well-defined standards. They diagnose your problem, present options, and formulate a plan. They're not trying to sell you anything other than their expertise. So, it's easy to place your trust in them and become teammates, often for life.

There are two big problems with how retirement preparation works now: 1) people aren't getting the financial advice they need, and 2) they aren't earning enough to save for retirement. The financial services industry can correct the first of these problems, but it requires some prioritizing and a commitment to change.

You'll recall that prior to 1980, most workers weren't responsible for their retirement because it was handled by employers, unions, or the government. Most people had no need for a financial advisor, so very few existed. People did occasionally need a stockbroker to help them buy shares if they had a little extra money to play with or got a hot tip.

On December 12, 1969, Loren Dunton convened a meeting of thirteen financial services industry leaders in Chicago to discuss the creation of a new profession. From that meeting came the International College for Financial Counseling, which included a membership association and an educational arm. The latter (called the College for Financial Planning) established a five-course curriculum leading to the CFP® designation. It graduated its first class in 1973. But with only thirty-five people in that class, not many people got help.[70]

When demand exceeds need, there's a rush to fill it. Eventually, "financial advisors" started popping up everywhere. But there were no national standards or requirements behind that title. It was like the Wild West. This isn't surprising. It was a new career, and it takes a long time to standardize a new career. Look at life coaches or fitness trainers. More

---

70   Lewis J. Walker, "The Profession of Financial Planning: Past, Present, and the Next 45 Years," Financial Planning Association, March 2018, https://www.financialplanningassociation.org/article/journal/MAR18-profession-financial-planning-past-present-and-next-45-years.

recently, look at artificial intelligence. Why isn't it regulated? Should it be regulated? Will regulation hamper its development? Everyone has an opinion, and at some point I'm sure we'll figure it out.

The time for the financial services industry to figure things out is now. Lots of people are angry and scared. My husband, Paul, and I were heading home from the Newark airport recently. Paul doesn't like to drive and I'm always working, so we hired a driver. Eddie was the nicest guy, and he started telling us his life story—how the company he worked for had eliminated his pension and now he had this chauffeuring job to make extra money and pay for his daughter's education. He didn't know what I did for a living, and he went on and on about how hard he'd worked his whole life. When his pension got frozen, the company offered him a 401(k), but he didn't understand how it worked and never signed up. Now he doesn't know if he'll ever be able to retire. Eddie, bless his heart, encapsulated this entire book. I gave him a big tip.

SURVEY *SAYS* — WHAT WAS YOUR BIGGEST CONCERN ABOUT HIRING A FINANCIAL ADVISOR?*

It would cost too much money = **41%**

I didn't have enough money to need a financial advisor = **28%**

I was afraid of feeling pressured = **15%**

I was afraid they'd criticize my financial situation = **8%**

*From a 2024 survey of 212 clients conducted by Evans Wealth Strategies

Eddie is the perfect example of financial needs not being met. There is so much more the industry can do to help Eddie and the millions like him. The CFP Board and other organizations are working hard. But imagine if each hospital in the United States set its own rules and regulations. It would be chaos. Like medicine, the financial services industry needs national coordination and oversight. Here are my suggestions for how we can better serve existing and potential clients and move the industry forward:

Standardize Titles

It should not be the client's job to figure out who's responsible and who's not. Why are there 253 financial designations in FINRA's database when FINRA clearly states that it doesn't approve or endorse any of these?

At the very least, there needs to be a national standard for the two most common titles: *financial advisor* and *financial planner*. As it is, anyone can use these titles regardless of their education and training level. Clients are handing over their entire life savings to these people. Meanwhile, we won't let someone fix an ingrown toenail without the proper credentials. How crazy is that? We've got to stop this free-for-all.

Shift from Selling to Advising

The industry needs to stop thinking of *financial advisor* as a sales job. The days of the stockbroker are gone. Clients want and need more holistic advice. So, if the type of advice is changing, the person giving the advice must change as well. Someone whose main skill is sales is probably not the best advisor. Research shows that clients desire a long-term relationship with their advisor and a financial plan for all aspects of their life.[71] They don't want another product. Accountants and lawyers aren't cold-calling people, so why in the world are we?

A popular expression in the financial services industry is "you eat what you kill." This means you're paid only on business you bring in. This is the definition of a salesperson. I've heard financial firms talk about shifting from selling investments to selling advice. But by continuing to use the word *selling*, we're creating an environment that attracts only salespeople. This is an enormous lost opportunity. While some salespeople can be great advisors, there are many good advisors who are lousy salespeople. This includes me and my staff!

Promote Behavioral Finance

In addition to being properly trained and certified, advisors need to have the right traits: morals above reproach, a desire to help others, great people skills, and an interest in financial planning and investments, in that order. They need to be *emotionally invested* in their clients. This is the realm of behavioral finance, and I believe it's the future. Human beings are emotional creatures, yet the financial services industry is reluctant to acknowledge this. It keeps rolling out the graphs and charts, not realizing that people don't make financial decisions based on graphs and charts. Many advisors are still more comfortable providing spreadsheets than empathy.

Behavioral finance fuses economics with psychology. Anyone embarking on a career as a financial advisor (and those who are already practicing) should get thoroughly trained in this. (My ABFP® certification is from the College for Financial Planning, but there are

---

71   Derek Lawson and Bradley Klontz, "Integrating Behavioral Finance, Financial Psychology, and Financial Therapy into the 6-Step Financial Planning Process," Financial Planning Association, July 2017, https://www.financialplanningassociation. org/article/journal/JUL17-integrating-behavioral-finance-financial-psychology-and-financial-therapy-6-step-financial.

other organizations offering similar ones.) When I give talks to other advisors, everyone wants to know my secret. It's simple (and it's not a secret!): behavioral finance.

Stop Explaining Everything

If my doctor explained everything that was going to happen during my surgery, I never would have had surgery. It would have scared the knickers off me. I don't need to go to medical school before I have an operation. Likewise, when you visit your CPA, they don't show you the tax law.

So, why does the financial services industry think people need to understand all the nuances of investment portfolios and planning for retirement? Because of the Big Lie. The government told people it was so simple they could do it themselves, and we're still operating on that principle when, in fact, it's *not* simple. After my forty-five years in finance, there are still things I don't understand. Obviously, it's important that clients understand their portfolios and the planning that's being done, but knowing the nuances of portfolio management and financial mathematics should not be the client's responsibility.

Insist on Fiduciary

The fiduciary rule means that the financial professional must put the client's needs before their own. Duh! Doctors take the Hippocratic oath and pledge to do no harm. While your physical health is important, so is your financial health. Anyone who tells you what to do with your money should be required to be a fiduciary. While it is a requirement for many, I believe it should be a requirement for all. It should not be one more thing a client has to figure out. (By the way, if an advisor is a CFP®, the CFP Board automatically requires them to act in accordance with the fiduciary standard.)

It is an honor and a privilege to do this job. I love my industry and the opportunity it affords me to help you. Nothing is more fulfilling than having clients I've worked with for years retire to the life they dreamed with financial security. But the need for these services is growing so fast, the industry and regulators can't keep pace. The old system needs tweaking. Obtaining financial advice and planning must become easier and safer for clients. Too many organizations within the industry are looking only at their small piece and not seeing the big picture. We need to work toward one consistent set of rules, regulations, and guidelines, because *that's* what's in the client's best interest.

One Last Story

June 2018. Rob was sixty-two, and his wife, Rita, was fifty-seven. They had never been to a financial advisor before. Rita was a schoolteacher and eligible for retirement. She wanted to retire as soon as possible. But they were nervous. So nervous. They had yanked all $750,000 of their savings out of the stock market after it dropped in the 2008–2009 financial crisis and never got back in. That money had been sitting in a low-interest account for the last ten years. Rita knew this was a bad idea and had pestered Rob to reinvest it, but he oversaw the money, and his fear had paralyzed him. A friend suggested they see me.

I ran the numbers. From 2009 through 2018, the S&P 500 returned over 11 percent. If they had stayed in the market, they would have earned $1,380,000. I did *not* tell them this. Hearing what they should have done would have made them feel worse. They needed to move forward.

Rob and Rita had been working on the things that didn't scare them—the things they understood. They had continued to save for retirement. Their house was almost paid off. They had no other debts and had bought life insurance. I did a full financial plan taking all these things into consideration, but it showed they wouldn't be able to retire for many years unless changes were made. Using plain English, I educated them about the market and how much it fluctuates. I convinced them to reinvest. The market was doing well, then the rug puller showed up: the pandemic of 2020 and the fastest stock market drop in history. We scheduled a Zoom call. We reviewed the plan. I reassured them that although I hadn't planned for a global pandemic, I had planned for market downturns. They had a fair amount of cash on hand, and the funds in the stock market weren't needed for a while. They didn't panic. They stuck with the plan.

Then we had the fastest stock market rise in history. Rita had continued working, but now she could retire at sixty-two. (Rob was working part time.) Then the rug puller showed up again. Rita died suddenly from a brain aneurysm the year she was set to retire. Rob was devastated. He came to see me to make sure he was going to be fine financially. He lamented that if he hadn't pulled out of the market, Rita could have retired at age fifty-seven and they would have had five fun years together. He knew the impact of his decision, but there was nothing left for me to offer other than empathy—and a hug.

Fear and the lack of a good financial advisor doesn't just cause you to lose money; it can cost you precious time with loved ones. It's been a few years, and I can tell Rob still misses Rita every day. (And I still miss Rita, too.) But he's able to live comfortably, and he has someone to call whenever he needs reassurance. That means a lot.

I get calls and meet with couples like Rob and Rita every week. There are so many people riding the roller coaster of life who need financial help but for a myriad of reasons either aren't seeking it or aren't getting it. My heart goes out to these folks. I wish I could help every one of you. But that's why I wrote this book. If I can't be there for you in person, I can be there for you through these pages.

Three Things to Remember from This Chapter

1. Behavioral finance fuses economics with psychology, and I believe it is the future.

2. Too many organizations within the industry are looking only at their small piece and not seeing the big picture.

3. We need to work toward one consistent set of rules, regulations, and guidelines, because *that's* what's in the client's best interest.

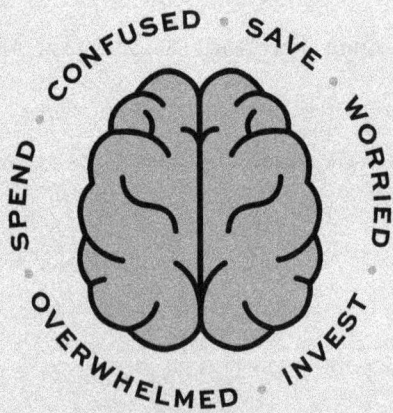

SPEND · CONFUSED · SAVE · WORRIED · INVEST · OVERWHELMED ·

MARYISMS

EVERYTHING I NEEDED TO KNOW, I LEARNED FROM FORTY YEARS IN FINANCE

A little bit of chocolate helps everything.

I like to think that everybody loves me; it's just that some of them haven't figured that out yet.

The stock market performs in a manner very similar to my weight—it goes up and down, but the trajectory is always up.

People aren't that interested in how much you know; they really want to know how much you care.

Your success in life isn't about what happens to you; it's about how you respond to it.

Instead of getting mad, try getting curious.

Most people are too worried thinking about themselves to really care about what you're doing.

Laughter is just as essential as food and water.

Stop seeking affirmation and start seeking information.

When you're in a hole, stop digging.

Bad things don't last forever, and neither do good things. So, make sure that when good things are happening, you enjoy them, and during the bad times, just hang on for a bit.

Asking questions is the best way to learn.

People will ask more questions when they understand what you're saying than when they don't.

The less people ask me about their money, the more nervous they are.

They fill libraries with things you don't know. Maybe go visit one.

Don't live your life performing for an imaginary audience.

Life is not about perfection. It's about progress.

Ask for help. People love helping other people. When someone can help you, it makes them feel really good about themselves.

Your opinion of me is none of my business.

Be kind to everyone, because everyone's dealing with something.

ACKNOWLEDGMENTS

To my husband, Paul Evans. Your love, kindness, patience, and humor feed my soul every day. You're always my biggest fan, even when I'm driving you crazy. This book never would have happened without you.

To my deceased parents (Margaret and George Clements). Your wisdom far exceeded your education. You taught me to fight for things that are worth fighting for, to never give up, and to look for the good in everything.

To my incredible staff: Crystal Dye, Sharon Stauffer, Michelle Tauber, Lori Bleamer, Maryann Baloh, Zach Long, Nicole Wescoe, and Richard "RJ" Whitelock. You make every day a pleasure and provided me with the time and space to write this book. I have complete trust in all of you.

A special thank you to Crystal. You are like a daughter to me. You trusted me in this crazy adventure and made it your life, too. You are always there for me. I don't know what I would do without you.

To my big, loving, and loud family:

My grandchildren—Zion, Ava, Isla, and Ben—and their mother, Nina. Dan will live on through you. The comfort that this brings me makes my heart sing.

My supportive stepfamily—Carol, Shawn, Paul Jr., Michael, Ayeisha, and Nathan. Your love and support held me up through the toughest times. My stepchildren—Jaiden, Apollo, Amara, and Savannah. You kids light up my world.

To my brothers, sisters, and in-laws—Peggy and Rich Jagodzin-ski, Jeanne Clements and Paul Richards, Jim and Kathy Clements, and Bill and Barb Clements. My talented and beautiful nieces and nephews—George Jagodzinski, Patrick Jagodzinski, Carolyn Conlee, Cindy Duhamel, Christina Clements, Michael Clements, William Clements, and Kathleen Perlman. I know that I can call on any of you when needed and you will be there. I am so lucky to have you in my life.

To my girlfriends—Susan Godbey, Denise Foley, Sara Altshul, Pam Boyer, Faith Wescoe, Jody King, Ann Kush, and too many others to name. You provide constant encouragement (although you think I'm smarter than I am).